all american

all american

a style book by

TOMMY HILFIGER
with DAVID A. KEEPS

A MADHOUSE PRODUCTION

UNIVERSE

A MADHOUSE PRODUCTION
PRODUCED BY B. JEFFREY MADOFF
CREATIVE DIRECTOR: DEREK UNGLESS
EDITORIAL DIRECTOR: GILLIAN YOUNG
PRODUCER OF PHOTOGRAPHY: PATRICK DEEDES-VINCKE

EDITOR: JAMES STAVE
PRODUCTION DIRECTOR: ELIZABETH WHITE

ART DIRECTOR: ALEX MIN
BOOK DESIGNER: MICHAEL ENGLISH AT ME DESIGN
COVER DESIGNER: TRACEY TANGO AT TOMMY HILFIGER

STILL-LIFE PHOTOGRAPHERS: BILL STEELE AND DAVID BASHAW
CLOTHING STYLISTS: DEBBI MASON AND ARABELLA GUNDRY-MILLS
PHOTOGRAPHIC RESEARCHERS: SHARI CHERTOK AND IAN SOUTHWOOD AT RE:SEARCH

First published in the United States of America in 1997
by UNIVERSE PUBLISHING
A Division of Rizzoli International Publications, Inc.
300 Park Avenue South
New York, NY 10010

97 98 99 00 01 / 10 9 8 7 6 5 4 3 2 1

Library of Congress Catalog Card Number: 97-61339

Printed in Japan

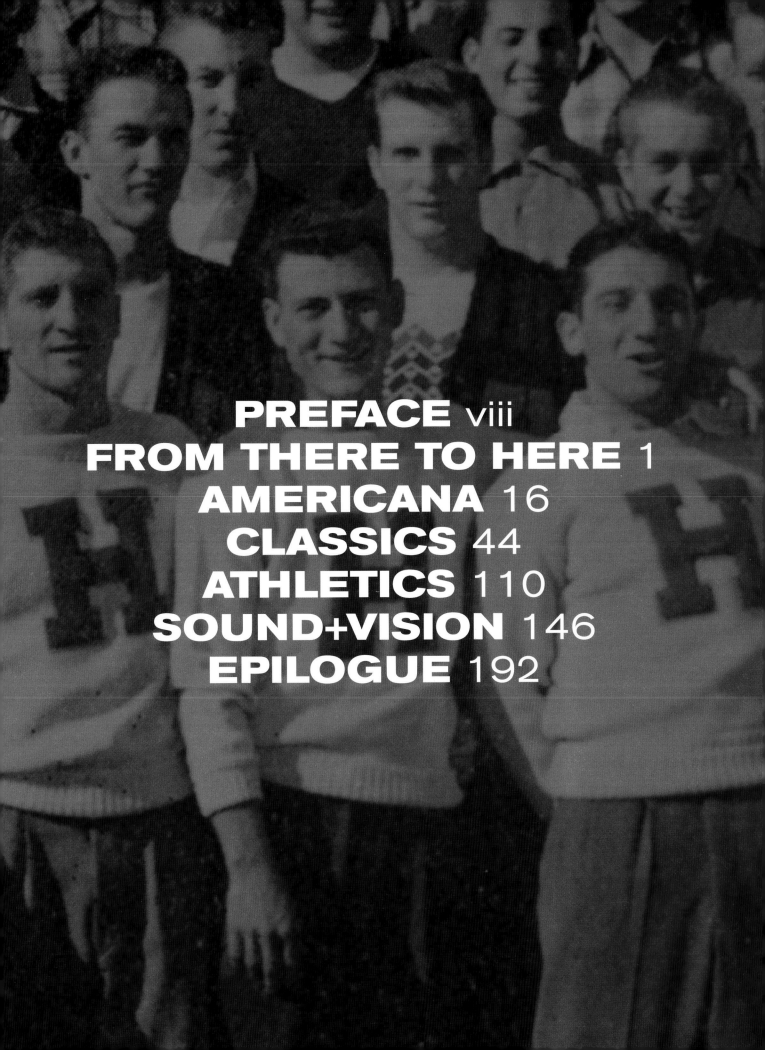

*Elmira heroes, left to right: Mark Twain;
Ernie Davis, All-American halfback from
Syracuse University and native of Elmira,
New York, won the Heisman Trophy in 1961,
but tragically, his promising future was cut
short by leukemia 18 months later; my
father, Richard Hilfiger*

WHEN IT CAME TIME TO PUT MY NAME ON A LINE OF CLOTHING, I LOOKED BACK TO THE BASICS I WAS BROUGHT UP WITH, THE CLEAN-CUT IVY LEAGUE LOOK OF THE EARLY SIXTIES. IN SOME VERY SIMPLE YET ELEGANT CLOTHING—BLAZERS AND SWEATERS FROM THE COLLEGE PLAYING FIELDS, CHINOS AND DENIMS FROM THE BLUE-COLLAR WORKFORCE—I FOUND A VOCABULARY OF COMFORTABLE, CASUAL DRESSING, THE ESSENCE OF AMERICAN SPORTSWEAR AND THE FOUNDATION OF POPULAR STYLE.

WE HAVE ARRIVED AT A UNIQUE MOMENT IN THE HISTORY OF MENSWEAR. WITH THE ADVENT OF CASUAL FRIDAYS, THE WORKPLACE HAS BECOME LESS FORMAL. OUR PREOCCUPATION WITH FITNESS AND SPORTS HAS MADE ATHLETIC CLOTHES ESSENTIAL WEEKEND WEAR. AND WE FREELY DRAW FROM THE FLASH AND GLAMOUR OF DECADES PAST TO BRIGHTEN UP OUR NIGHTS OUT ON THE TOWN. IN SOME WAYS, WE ARE MOVING BEYOND FASHION TO A CELEBRATION OF PERSONAL STYLE. FASHION IS FOR THE MOMENT, BUT STYLE IS INNATE AND ENDURING. PEOPLE WITH STYLE AND GOOD TASTE NEVER HAVE TO TRY TOO HARD. YOU CAN WEAR A T-SHIRT WITH A PAIR OF JEANS, A PAIR OF SOCKS, AND TENNIS SNEAKERS AND LOOK ABSOLUTELY PERFECT.

THIS BOOK IS A VOYAGE THROUGH THE CULTURAL CHANGES THAT HAVE SHAPED FASHION, AND THE FASHIONS THAT HAVE SHAPED OUR CULTURE FROM THE 1950S TO TODAY. IT IS A PERSONAL JOURNEY THROUGH THE ELEMENTS OF STYLE THAT HAVE INFLUENCED MY WARDROBE AND FORMED MY DESIGN SENSIBILITY. THINK OF THIS BOOK AS A REFERENCE GUIDE, A WAY TO UNDERSTAND WHERE FASHION COMES FROM AND WHERE IT'S GOING. SEE HOW THE IMAGES OF THE PAST RESONATE IN THE PRESENT, HOW YOU CAN PUT TOGETHER A MODERN WARDROBE THAT SUITS YOUR LIFESTYLE BY USING TAILORED CLOTHES AND SPORTY GEAR. LET THIS BOOK BE AN INSPIRATION EVERY TIME YOU OPEN YOUR CLOSET.

IN PREPARING THIS BOOK I WOULD LIKE TO EXPRESS THANKS TO SUSIE, MY WIFE AND BEST FRIEND OF 18 YEARS, WHO TAUGHT ME NEVER TO SETTLE AND ALWAYS TO SEEK PERFECTION, WHICH IS WHY WE MAKE SUCH A GREAT TEAM. SHE IS MY INSPIRATION. AND TO MY FAVORITE ASSETS IN THE WORLD, MY CHILDREN: ABBY, WHO TELLS ME WHAT TO WEAR SO I DON'T LOOK LIKE A NERD; RICHARD JAMES, WHO LIKES TO BE CALLED KING RICHARD JAMES—HE DOES NOT UNDERSTAND WHY HE SHOULD HAVE TO WEAR FANCY CLOTHES AT TIMES AND WISHES I MADE TOYS; ELIZABETH (FOO FOO), WHO IS MY 5:30 A.M. WAKEUP CALL AND WOULD RATHER BE A BOY; AND KATHLEEN, MY MASCOT AT HOME, WHO MOST RESEMBLES HER DAD. I WOULD ALSO LIKE TO THANK MY FATHER, RICHARD, AND MY MOTHER, VIRGINIA, FOR BRINGING ME INTO THIS LIFE AND SUPPORTING ALL MY WILD DREAMS, AND MY EIGHT BROTHERS AND SISTERS: KATHLEEN (KATHY), DOROTHY (SUSIE), ELIZABETH (BETSY), WILLIAM (BILLY), ROBERT (BOBBY), MARIE (DEE DEE), ANDREW (ANDY), VIRGINIA (GINNY). SPECIAL THANKS TO GINNY FOR BEING SUCH AN IMPORTANT PART OF MY DESIGN TEAM AND ANDY FOR CONNECTING ME TO THE MUSIC WORLD. THANKS TO AUNT ANNIE FOR TEACHING ME TO DO MY BEST IN EVERYTHING I DO. TO MY PARTNER SILAS CHOU, WHO FOUND ME IN BEVERLY HILLS AND BELIEVED IN ME; LAWRENCE STROLL, WHO TAUGHT ME HOW TO THINK BIG; AND JOEL HOROWITZ, MY ROCK OF GIBRALTAR. AND THANKS TO MIKE AND JOE, MICHAEL H. AND BUBBLES. THANKS TO MY ELMIRA CONTINGENCY, MY FRIENDS FOR 40-PLUS YEARS: FRENCHY, SPANGS, BLOOMER, RATSY, K.D., THE COLGIES, AND PAPPY. SPECIAL THANKS TO MY FORMER PARTNER LARRY STEMERMAN FROM PEOPLE'S PLACE AND HIS ENTIRE FAMILY FOR THEIR TREMENDOUS SUPPORT IN THE EARLY DAYS. I WOULD ALSO LIKE TO THANK MY LAWYER AND CONFIDANT TOM CURTIN AND HIS ASSOCIATE JOE LAMASTRA FOR THEIR ADVICE AND CONSULTATION. AND I CANNOT FORGET MOHAN MURJANI, WHO BELIEVED IN ME; STU KOMER, WHO FINALLY PERSUADED ME TO LEAVE ELMIRA; ANGELO, EMIL, AND ALEX FOR MAKING NEW YORK FUN. IT IS ALSO IMPORTANT TO THANK MY WONDERFUL AND DEDICATED STAFF AT TOMMY HILFIGER WHO HAVE HELPED ME REALIZE MY DREAMS AND HAVE BECOME PART OF MY FAMILY. UNFORTUNATELY, THERE ARE TOO MANY NAMES TO NAME, BUT I KNOW YOU KNOW WHO YOU ARE. SPECIAL THANKS TO QUINCY JONES, RUSSELL SIMMONS, MICK JAGGER, PETE TOWNSHEND, AND DAVID BOWIE. AND TO THE TEAM WHO PUT THIS BOOK TOGETHER WITH ME: CHARLES MIERS OF UNIVERSE PUBLISHING, JEFF MADOFF, DEREK UNGLESS, GILLIAN YOUNG, PATRICK DEEDES-VINCKE, JIM STAVE AND DAVID A. KEEPS.

FROM THERE TO HERE

I was born in Elmira, a small town in upstate New York. I'm a third-generation American.

My father's ancestors are from Bavaria—part Dutch and part German. My mother is English, Irish, and Scottish. Growing up in Elmira was sort of like living in "Leave It to Beaver–land." Everyone knew each other, and all the neighbors were very close. Our doors were always open, never locked. People would just come and go as they pleased; you trusted everybody. My mom still lives in the same house I grew up in. The house has five bedrooms, and our family had nine children. So figure out the math! We teamed up together, learned how to share, and how to respect one another—and we are all still very close. My mother taught us the golden rule: Do unto others as you would have them do unto you.

Just imagine five girls and four boys under one roof. Our house really rattled. All the boys loved music; the girls loved clothes. My parents were very open and liberal. We had sleepovers and slumber parties. In the basement we'd have band practice. In the backyard we'd have baseball practice. The driveway would be full of kids on bicycles, and my sisters would be in one of the bedrooms playing with Barbie. We had a cat named Barney and a dog named Garnet.

I played Little League baseball, small-fry football, went ice skating and skiing with the family. I loved collecting sports equipment—baseball gloves, bats, football helmets, shoulder pads. And, of course, I needed my six-shooters—every boy has his guns—and chaps and cowboy hats. And I had to have a Davy Crockett coonskin cap. Every little boy wanted to look like this

ELMIRA
NEW YORK
THE GLIDER CAPITAL OF AMERICA

hero. As I can attest, the concept of people dressing to look like their heroes is not new at all: I used to wear Billy the Kid–brand jeans.

I loved Roy Rogers and Sky King, all the American favorites. I read mysteries, the Hardy Boys and Nancy Drew, and I read about Tom Sawyer and Huck Finn because Mark Twain had kept a summer house in Elmira and was a local hero. I was in Cub Scouts and Boy Scouts, but not seriously—I didn't like it: I liked the scout uniforms and pocketknives, but not the discipline of scouting. I'm dyslexic, so I couldn't tie those damn knots. I would look at the diagrams and stare at the rope and I just didn't get it. When somebody tried to show me how to do it, I just got frustrated.

Christmas was very "storybook." On Christmas morning we would wake up and run downstairs, thinking Santa Claus had really been there. Over the years, I got a red bicycle, a red truck, airplanes, cowboy hats, a football—all the traditional Christmas presents. And I got marionettes, which I loved. I played with them until I was 11 or 12. Of course, I liked the Howdy Doody Show because Howdy was a marionette. Then someone told me I looked like Howdy Doody—after that I never watched the show again.

When I was very young, my favorite program was the Mickey Mouse Club. I was in love with Annette Funicello. I always wanted a Mickey Mouse hat with real Mickey Mouse ears, and finally I got one for my birthday. I wore it everywhere, but one day I dropped it in the toilet. I was so upset, I didn't stop crying until my mother took it out, rinsed it off, and ironed it so the ears would stay up.

We were a totally American family. We drove around in a Ford Country Squire station wagon and my dad would drive fast. This was before cars came with seat belts, so I'd be sliding all over the front seat. He'd go slamming the gas pedal into the floor, come right up to a stop light, and then hit the brakes. We ate all the American grocery-store brands: Campbell's soup, Jiffy peanut butter and Welch's grape jelly on Sunbeam bread, Ritz crackers, Ring Dings, Hostess Twinkies, and Snickers, Milky Way, and Hershey bars. In the summer we'd have barbecues: hot dogs, potato chips, Coca-Cola, potato salad with Hellmann's mayonnaise.

Watching Ozzie and Harriet was a family ritual. On Sunday night we'd gather in front of the TV set and watch the Wonderful World of Disney, with movies like OLD YELLER, and of course we'd watch the Ed Sullivan Show. I remember when the Beatles came on. My sisters and brothers and I thought they were the coolest; my parents thought they were obnoxious, with that moppy, floppy hair. TV played a big role in my life then. I loved The Twilight Zone. Rod Serling was Ivy League all the way, but with a slicker look. I loved The Fugitive, Bonanza, and western movies. The show I have the worst memories of was Lawrence Welk, which I will always associate with my parents getting ready to go out on Saturday nights and my having to stay behind.

My dad worked in a jewelry store, fixing watches and jewelry, and my mother was a nurse. They were very cautious about spending money and very proud. They didn't spoil our fun, but they had their rules. They didn't want us ever to use bad manners, get in trouble, do poorly in school, have long hair, or leave our bicycles on the front lawn. They tried to be very buttoned up about the whole thing. Even though they both worked a lot, it seemed like we were always broke, down to our last dime. It was stressful, and therefore I cherished having a job, not having to ask my father for money, being able to buy my own clothes.

Having a job also meant I could pay for my own haircuts. Going to the barber cost $1.25 back then, so my father used to sit my brothers and me down on a high chair in the kitchen on a Sunday night, put the sheet around our necks, turn on clippers, and say, "Hold still." While a lot of other kids had

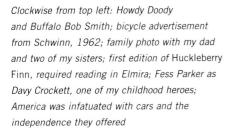

*Clockwise from top left: Howdy Doody
and Buffalo Bob Smith; bicycle advertisement
from Schwinn, 1962; family photo with my dad
and two of my sisters; first edition of* Huckleberry
Finn, *required reading in Elmira; Fess Parker as
Davy Crockett, one of my childhood heroes;
America was infatuated with cars and the
independence they offered*

It was sort of like living in

'Leave It to Beaver–land.'

CUBBY

JIMMIE

KAREN

One of my favorite TV programs was the Mickey Mouse Club, with Jimmie Dowd and the Mousketeers

haircuts where the sides were cut but there was still something on top, I was buzzed all over. During the early Beatles period, I started to grow it out in front a little bit, and a bit more, and then a bit more. Finally, when I could pay for my own haircut, I didn't let my father do it anymore.

My first job, at age nine, was mowing lawns. It was buggy and hot and terrible. At ten, I had a newspaper route. When I was 14, I got a job at Pal's Sporting Goods, at $1.25 an hour as a stock boy. Mr. Paltrowitz, the owner, taught me everything there was to know about sporting goods and how to operate a retail business. That's where I fell in love with sports equipment. When I was 16, I got a job at a Hess service station. When a customer pulled in, we'd run up to the car and ask them if they wanted us to fill it up. We had to wash the windows and check the oil whether they wanted us to or not. I made $2.50 an hour, which was a lot in those days, and I got to work with older kids. I remember feeling very proud wearing my uniform with the big Hess logo on the back. Ever since, the graphics of the automobile world has been an influence on my designs.

In those days I was very interested in clothing, particularly the Ivy League look: chinos, madras, oxford cloth shirts. I had all the grooming stuff too: Old Spice, Canoë, English Leather, Jade East, Wildroot, Brylcreem, Vitalis. I wanted to look rich, and I wanted to look cool because I was always very small for my age. People used to say, "Oh, isn't he cute?" I didn't want people to refer to me as a little boy. I wanted to be a teenager, but I wasn't quite there. Until I was 18, people didn't think I was even 15. I didn't shave; I didn't even have whiskers until I was 17. I wanted to grow sideburns so badly. After all, this was the sixties.

I mostly wanted to look my age because I was interested in girls. Courtship was pretty uncomplicated back then. There was a local radio station, WENY, 1200 AM, that played a lot of Motown and used to have record hops. In those days the boys really didn't like to dance. It was boys on one side, girls on the other. There were a few people who danced, but it wasn't the cool thing to do. Later on, when we got driver's licenses, we used to go to drive-in movies. I vaguely remember some of the films we saw, but we were really there to drink, make out with girls, and smoke cigarettes.

I think my high school friends thought I would never make it. I was always in trouble with teachers, parents, and friends, always into mischief—my friends used to call me Eddie Haskell when they introduced me to their parents—not severely illegal mischief, but I skipped school a lot and caused trouble with my friends' parents. The minute I got my driver's license, I bought my own car—a 1960 Olds '98. After driving it for a while, I decided I really wanted a Volkswagen Beetle, so I traded my Olds for an old beat-up Beetle. Since it was completely rusted, I painted it olive drab.

When I was 17 years old, I went to Cape Cod with my friends to hang out. I got a job at a boutique in Hyannis. It was a sort of poster, incense, candles, and flower shop called the Sunflower, with Hendrix, Jefferson Airplane, Blind Faith playing in the background, the smell of incense, the glare of psychedelic colors everywhere, and strobe lights. The dress was sandals, bell bottoms, long hair. I was into it all. One of my icons at the time was the poster for the surfing film THE ENDLESS SUMMER. That was the first time I had ever been away from home alone, and it was really the summer of the beginning of my new life.

When I came back from Cape Cod I had much longer hair than when I left, and my father was just shaking his head, no way. My parents did not want to hear about it. They were a combination of June and Ward Cleaver and the image you see in the Norman Rockwell painting of the guy in the station wagon with the kids and dogs. When I came back that summer, my father did not want even to look at me. My friends all had long hair, too, and we were all into dressing really mod. After school we'd go to my basement, or to one of my friends' houses, to listen to the Who and the Stones and the Beatles.

We were in our senior year in high school. Every morning one of my friends, Larry Stemerman, would come to my house to pick me up for school, and we would look at each other and say, "Do you really feel like going today?" "No." So we'd go to Ithaca, a college town with cool people, boutiques, record shops, and a lot of activity. We found a head shop selling bell bottoms, and we started talking to the people who ran the store, and I said, "Wow, can we buy these from you and sell them to our friends?"—which is exactly what we ended up doing. Then Larry and I and our friend Jon Allen came up with the idea of opening our own business. I had saved $150, Larry had $150, and Jon had $150. We opened a shop in Elmira called People's Place, painted the walls black, burned incense, played music, and sold candles and bell bottoms. It was a fun place where all the cool people came in and hung out. The music was loud, the incense was burning, it was a great place to be for young people at that time.

Business got very good. I thought, "This is unbelievable." And then business started getting even better. We opened another store, and then another after another, all throughout upstate New York college towns. Larry's father, who owned a shoe store, was very helpful in guiding us into becoming official retailers. And my father was a bit more tolerant after he saw that I could make something of myself. In the beginning, I did just about everything creative myself. I redecorated the store and the windows on a regular basis, I romanced and displayed the merchandise, sold it, rang it up on the register, wrapped it, and walked the customers to the door. But I wasn't really happy with what we were selling. And I thought maybe I should be designing the merchandise too. I wanted the clothes to be cooler, so I began sketching my own ideas

Above: I still treasure my varsity jacket from my high school days at Elmira Free Academy; facing page: freshman-class yearbook photo, 1967; advertisements for grooming essentials (R. Kravette, Jericho, NY/used with permission of the Procter & Gamble Company; © 1963 Bristol-Myers, reproduced with permission of the Bristol-Myers Squibb Company)

The Endless Summer

A true motion picture about surfing.
Filmed in Africa, Australia, New Zealand, Tahiti, Hawaii and California.
A BRUCE BROWN FILM IN COLOR

Distributed by Cinema V

WOODSTOCK
MUSIC & ART FAIR
presents
AN
AQUARIAN
EXPOSITION
in
WHITE LAKE, N.Y.

3 DAYS of PEACE & MUSIC

AUGUST 15, 16, 17.

Larry Stemerman (from left), Tom Hilfiger and John Allen, owners of The People's Pla

Bell Bottom Business Booming

'Mod, Mod World' for 3 Youths

By DICK MITCHELL

"To the old, anything new is bad news."

This is the philosophy of three "mod" youths—Larry Stemerman of 86 Greenridge Drive, Thomas Hilfiger of 606 W. Clinton St. and John Allen of 600 Cornell Road, all seniors at Elmira Free Academy.

They parlayed a $400 investment into a thriving downtown business known as the People's Place.

Despite their profit making venture the long-haired, mod dressed youth say they have not joined "the establishment"—nor are they fighting it.

Stemerman said that as proof, the three youths aren't conforming to the established procedures of business.

• • •

"What business would hire youths with long hair?" he asked. "We're not white collar conservatives."

Other youths describe the People's Place as more of an experience than a chore— what with the odor of incense, leather and suede and sounds of the latest records.

Discussing this environment

Hilfiger commented, "The members of the establishment are committed to their generation and we're servants to ours."

"I'm my own boss," added Allen. "I don't have the hassles older, established store workers and bosses have, because of my age.

Long-haired mods sometimes are harassed by the older generation, the three agree, "because they think this makes us degenerates."

• • •

Stemerman recalled that he and Hilfiger recently sat at a coffee shop next to two women.

"Do you have jobs?" one of the women asked the two boys.

The other woman laughed and commented: "Who would hire them with hair like that?"

Hilfiger recalls that at this point they told the two women they owned their own business. "It really blew their minds," he said with a chuckle.

He said it will be necessary for his generation to suffer disrespect and humiliation

from older persons until th discover that "some you really have something go for them."

• • •

The three plan coll educations but will wait u they consider themsel mature enough for the perience.

"Kids are rushed into c lege when they are mature enough to understa the responsibility of a coll education," Stemerman c tends.

Who would buy a pair striped bell bottoms, Pe Fonda glasses, white l body shirts, flutes or str candles?

Quite a few people woul

For example, since th opened Dec. 1, they have s more than 300 pairs of b bottoms and more than body shirts.

They say that the ent stock has been sold th times and their investm has grown 10 times.

During the Christm season they averaged $500 day in sales.

They are doing so we they have enlarged the st to twice its original size.

people's place

and found a manufacturer that could make apparel to my specifications.

The best moment was in 1972, when we were informed that there was a risk of heavy flooding. Our store was on a lower level, so Larry and I moved all the merchandise from the basement to the top floor of the building. Elmira was soon flooded under 30 feet of water. There wasn't a stitch of merchandise left in the entire city. People were out of their homes with no food, no clothes, no furniture. We were the only people with merchandise left. So we sold all this funky clothing to little old ladies and all different types of people. The Red Cross gave them money to get back on their feet, so they came to the store and bought our bell bottoms, beaded blouses, crochet vests, and patchwork leather jackets. All of Elmira was dressed in super-cool clothes. If you were passing through, you'd have thought you were on Carnaby Street. Everyone was dressed to the nines.

Eventually I started losing interest in the store. When I was 25, it went bankrupt. It was very sobering. I paid off my debt and went back into business, but it was never the same. I ended up selling my shares in the stores a few years later. I think you have to learn from your mistakes. You also have to just dive into something you believe in.

People's Place also brought me the love of my life, Susan Cirona, whom I met when she got an after-school job at the boutique in Ithaca. I'd just come back from a trip to London. I had very long hair, platforms, all the cool, mod gear and jewelry from the Kensington Market. To Susie, I looked like some overblown spectacle, a creature on a total rock-star trip. Eventually, she became less afraid of me when she figured I wasn't from Mars, and we became very close. She was remarkably creative, and I thought we could make a great team. We decided to move to New York City and to look for design work. Susie and I had a working honeymoon in Bombay, where we designed clothes for our new company, Tommy Hill.

When we returned, we joined Jordache Jeans, but they didn't understand what we were trying to do, and we were basically out on the streets. I was knocking on doors every day looking for design work. As I had only two months of official experience, at Jordache, I decided the only way to overcome this would be to create my own company. Eventually, I met a clothing-factory owner who was making fuddy-duddy women's clothes and whom I persuaded to start a more contemporary line. We began 20th Century Survival, which was all military gear with swashbuckler shirts, very new wave. Then at the height of the Japanese fashion craze in 1982, Susie started O'Tokyo and I started Click Point, both of us doing very architectural women's clothing, mine inspired by David Bowie's "China Girl" period.

We had our first child in 1985, so I was considering taking a steady design job with either Calvin Klein or Perry Ellis. I had offers from both, and I was completely confused about which to go with. In desperation I called a psychic named Zvia, whom we had met in Los Angeles, from a pay phone on Seventh Avenue and 40th Street. Zvia dismissed my concerns. "But you don't understand," I insisted. "This is CALVIN and PERRY. These are fashion ICONS." "Hold on, something better will be coming," Zvia intoned. And the next day I was called to a meeting with Murjani, who offered me my own company. That was the same week I got a summons for jumping the turnstiles in the subway. We were three months behind in the rent, and I had no money. By then I knew what I really wanted to do. My vision turned full circle from the trendy clothes of the eighties back to my preppy roots. Picturing a more New England, outdoorsy, and classic campus look that I knew would last, I launched Tommy Hilfiger.

AMERICANA

Whenever I look at the Statue of Liberty, the Empire State Building, Mt. Rushmore, whenever I see a pair of blue jeans or a '65 Mustang, I realize that these are all icons that make me proud to be American.

The history of our country has always been about vast, progressive changes in society and in the way people live. I think we all recognize that there are shortcomings to the system, but as a nation we hold ourselves up to an ideal. I think Americans are proud of their country and their lives and honest about their desires: a lot of people take it for granted that we live in this bliss, to which many others look yearningly as a dreamland. We have generous living standards, a treasury of music and art, a bounty of style and fashion, and a lot of freedom and enthusiasm within our lives. We have spontaneity, but we also have rules to protect us.

America's finest metaphor always has been, and always will be, that it is one great big melting pot. I love that idea. I like things to be mixed-up—not confused, but diverse. There are all different types of people in this American melting pot: gay, straight, black, white, Hispanic, Asian—all making up a whole that gives American life its incredible vibrancy. Maybe my love for the mix comes from having so many brothers and sisters, all with different personalities. And even though Elmira, the town where I was raised, only had some 40,000 people, there were all types.

Growing up in a middle-class, white-bread neighborhood of numerous Irish Catholic families with a lot of kids, I knew there were traditional values to absorb as well as a world full of modern products to fall in love with. There were hot dogs, baseball, and apple pie. TV and rock and roll. The game I didn't really understand was that of the rich. Mysterious to me were certain well-to-do, old-world families that I delivered newspapers to: I would see more than one car in the driveway or a swimming pool in the backyard; a maid would answer the door; the family would take vacations in Florida or the Bahamas or go away for the whole summer. Sometimes when I'd go to the door to collect for the paper, the mother would be all dressed up in the middle of the day.

That was just one part of the America I grew up with—the American Dream. At school there were rich kids, but there were also hoods and jocks and preppies. The preppy group was much more cool to be in; you could still get up to all kinds of mischief, but because you looked Ivy League you weren't suspected of being a troublemaker. Then there was the black crowd. They were into really cool stuff, music and sports, and they had a way about them that interested me. It was almost mysterious, a culture that I had never been exposed to in a respectful way.

Today, of course, we all know each other better. America has seemingly gone from a simple Norman Rockwell–esque existence to a much more sophisticated, cosmopolitan life. In a way, it's like SATURDAY EVENING POST or READER'S DIGEST versus VANITY FAIR or HARPER'S BAZAAR. Everybody now is in tune with what is glamorous; everybody knows what's hip. Instead of going to play bingo in church, you may just as easily be heading off to some video-awards ceremony. Switch on MTV and you'll see hip-hop kids and punk rockers of every color, all wearing the same funky shoes. Hang out in Miami Beach and see Rollerbladers zipping down Ocean Drive past outdoor cafés filled with stylish people. It's a fashion exposition 24 hours a day. A lot of these fashions have a pedigree. Look at the kids in Seattle wearing flannel shirts to rock shows—they're the same kind of shirts that people have worn to go camping and hunting in New England for years. Go out to a club in New York and there are guys that look like they came out of a midwestern country club in the early sixties or dropped in straight from a California beach. All of this is now American style.

American fashion designers are forever going off to Europe, all over the world for that matter, but European fashion has been the leading source of inspiration for American designers. Not so long ago, however, we began to see European designers turning out the classic all-American look—khakis, varsity jackets, hiking boots, and the like—but with a uniquely European interpretation. Then we brought it back and did it another way. And now they're all copying our urban hip-hop street looks, but with a different flavor. This is how fashion works: we'll take ideas from them, and they'll take them back, like one big game of ping-pong.

When I started to travel the world, I saw the fruits of American labor everywhere I went, the products and logos that are the trademarks of our industry and our culture. In the most exotic places in the world, you will see people wearing Levi's and drinking Coca-Cola, obsessing over fifties cars, and sporting cowboy shirts and boots, or wearing the rugged clothes we make for the great outdoors. No matter how different the customs, the world is tuned in to the signature emblems of the American lifestyle.

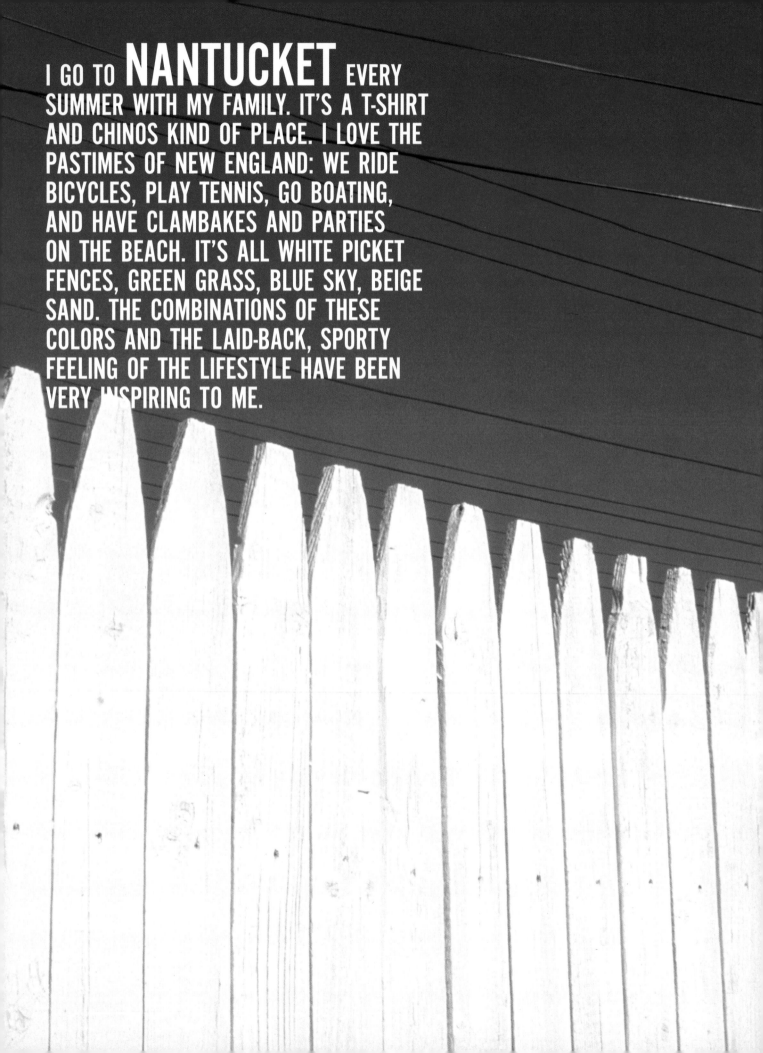

I GO TO **NANTUCKET** EVERY SUMMER WITH MY FAMILY. IT'S A T-SHIRT AND CHINOS KIND OF PLACE. I LOVE THE PASTIMES OF NEW ENGLAND: WE RIDE BICYCLES, PLAY TENNIS, GO BOATING, AND HAVE CLAMBAKES AND PARTIES ON THE BEACH. IT'S ALL WHITE PICKET FENCES, GREEN GRASS, BLUE SKY, BEIGE SAND. THE COMBINATIONS OF THESE COLORS AND THE LAID-BACK, SPORTY FEELING OF THE LIFESTYLE HAVE BEEN VERY INSPIRING TO ME.

IT IS ALSO VERY DETAILED—YOU SEE EVERY LITTLE THREAD

IS VERY GENUINE, BUT ALSO HAS A REAL SENSE OF HUMOR.

AND ZIPPER—BUT NOT EVERYTHING YOU SEE IS PERFECT.

U.S.A. SOME OF THEM WERE RE-CREATED IN MY OWN FAMILY.

Going and Coming, *Norman Rockwell*
Saturday Evening Post, *August 30, 1947*

THREW A FEW MORE KIDS IN THE BACK, THAT COULD'VE BEEN US.

AMERICA IS A **CAR** CULTURE. WE'RE IN LOVE WITH TRAVEL AND ALL OF ITS TRAPPINGS, FROM TRUCK-STOP DINERS TO CAR COATS. AS SOON AS I GOT MY LICENSE, I WAS READY TO HIT THE ROAD.

Route 66. Photograph by Andreas Feininger, 1953

The Car Coat

An American classic comes of age

The car has always influenced fashion. It's considered a fait accompli that JFK's bare head was solely responsible for the plunge in hat sales in the sixties, but in fact it was the lowering of the automobile's roofline in the late fifties that lowered the book on the hat industry—there just wasn't enough headroom to wear a hat in the newly streamlined car.

Driving has had an effect on hemlines too. The full-length motoring coat, known as the duster, was needed at the turn of the century to shield the driver from dirt and detritus spewed up around the open-carriage Ford Model-T. The shorter-length car coat, virtually a uniform for the station-wagon set of the fifties, was a hip- to three-quarter-length sport or utility coat made in a variety of fabrics (wool, cotton, corduroy) with a fly-front buttoning and a fur or pile spread collar that simply afforded greater ease in sliding in and out of the vehicle (and made for a more comfortable ride). The term "car coat" has come to mean any coat of shorter length. The duster was briefly revived as a fashion item in the new-wave eighties. Matt Dillon wore a variation in DRUGSTORE COWBOY. His, of course, was leather.

Fifties car coat. Photograph by Bill Steele

In the fifties, everything was aerodynamic, from Elvis Presley's hair to the fins of a Cadillac. The jazzy styling of old cars is pure Americana, and the shapes and colors continue to exert their influence on fashion.

Tailfins, *Westchester County, New York. Photograph by Elliott Erwitt, 1957*

The Tailfin

Design classics for the auto-motivated

BUICK CENTURY   year: 1955   original cost: $2,601

CADILLAC ELDORADO BROUGHAM   year: 1957   original cost: $5,048

CHEVROLET IMPALA   year: 1958   original cost: $2,693

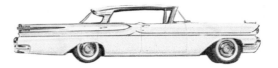

MERCURY MONTCLAIR   year: 1958   original cost: $3,248

CADILLAC FLEETWOOD   year: 1960   original cost: $9,533

FORD FAIRLANE VICTORIA   year: 1956   original cost: $2,294

CHRYSLER NEWPORT   year: 1962   original cost: $3,027

DE SOTO FIREDOME CONVERTIBLE   year: 1956   original cost: $3,052

I LOOK AT **COWBOY** SHIRTS AS TREASURES, THE ONES WITH PEAR

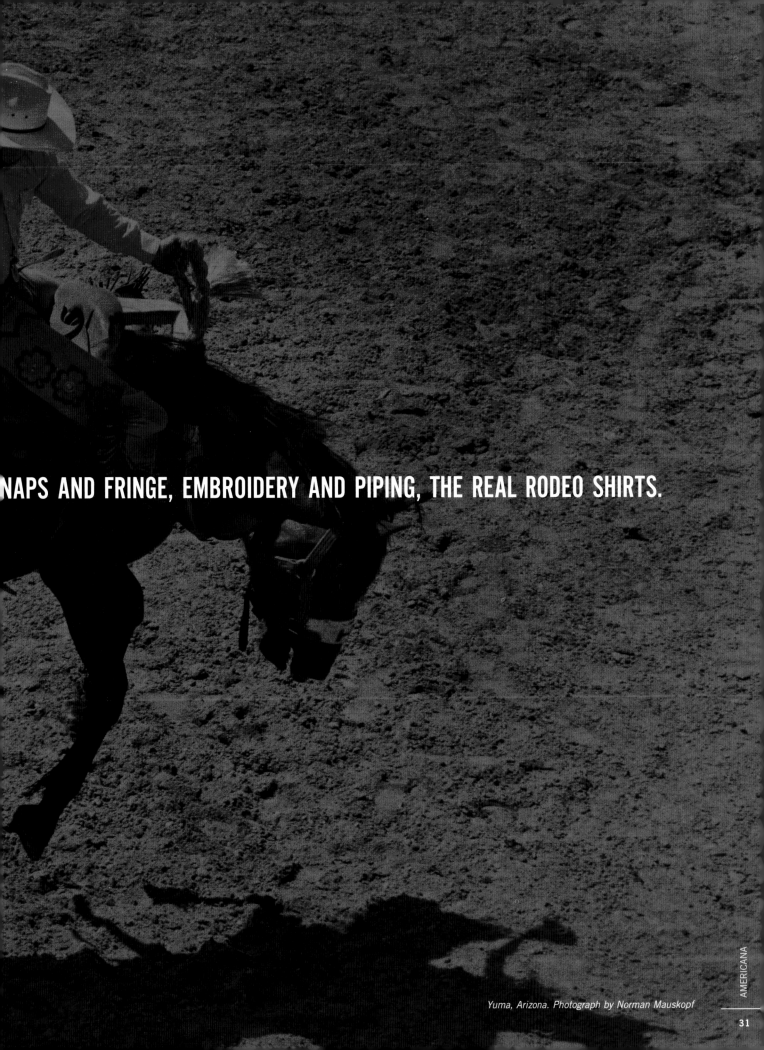

NAPS AND FRINGE, EMBROIDERY AND PIPING, THE REAL RODEO SHIRTS.

Yuma, Arizona. Photograph by Norman Mauskopf

ZX Ranch, Paisley, Oregon. *Photograph by Kurt Markus, 1981*

Roy Rogers

Jon Voight in Midnight Cowboy, 1969

Western clothes have their own sense of style. Sometimes they're rough and rugged; sometimes they're dressy and all duded up. The way cowboy shirts look best is with either completely unwashed denims or terribly beat-up jeans.

Gloria Winters and Kirby Grant from the TV show Sky King

John Travolta in Urban Cowboy, 1980

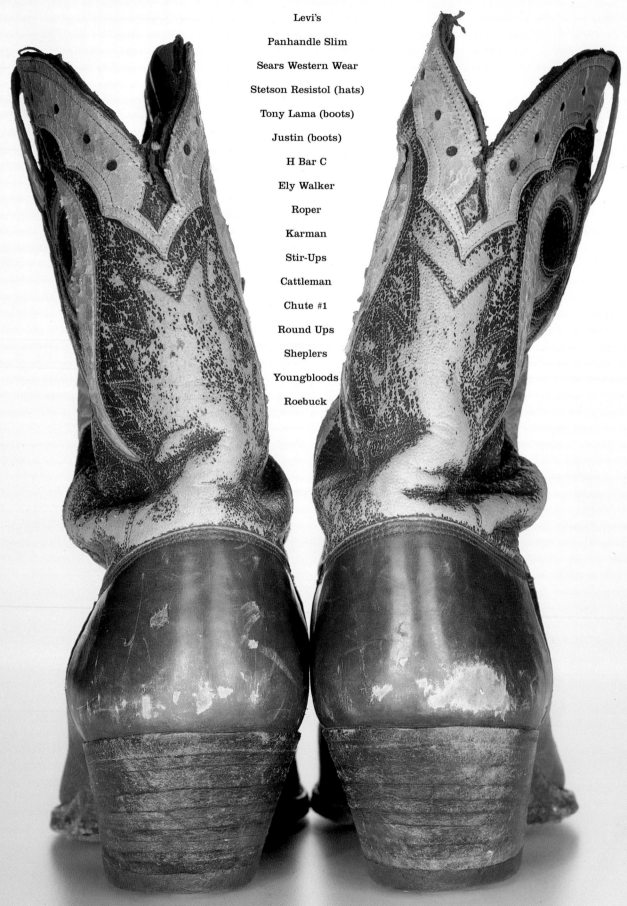

AUTHENTIC WESTERN

The brands buckaroos wear

Wrangler

Levi's

Panhandle Slim

Sears Western Wear

Stetson Resistol (hats)

Tony Lama (boots)

Justin (boots)

H Bar C

Ely Walker

Roper

Karman

Stir-Ups

Cattleman

Chute #1

Round Ups

Sheplers

Youngbloods

Roebuck

Vintage cowboy boots and shirt. Photographs by Bill Steele

THE YOKE
On the front and back of the shoulders; has a double thickness of fabric to provide extra protection from the sun.

BANDANNA
Sometimes added to the outfit to protect cowboys' noses and mouths from wind and dust during cattle drives.

FRINGE
A decorative hangover from the era when buckskin cowboy jackets were fringed to help water roll off the garment during rainstorms.

POCKETS
The slanted, besom pocket jauntily mirrors the shape of the yoke and is finished with embroidery that reinforces the corners.

SNAPS
Take the place of buttons, because they don't tear off during rough riding chores on the range or at the rodeo. The fanciest, made of pearl, were developed in the late forties.

THE SLEEVE
Gauntlet cuffs add extra flash.

PIPING
Another decorative element that separates the fancy rodeo shirt from everyday work wear.

THERE'S NOTHING AS INVIGORATINGLY AMERICAN AS A DAY IN **THE GREAT OUTDOORS.** WHEN I WAS A CHILD, WE WOULD GO ON PICNICS TO THE FINGER LAKES. ALL THE KIDS WOULD BE RUNNING AROUND, SWIMMING, OUT IN ROWBOATS AND MAHOGANY CANOES.

Lake Placid, Adirondack Mountains

GROMMETS
Provide ventilation at the neckline.

SHOULDER
Quilted appliqué provides an extra layer of protection when shooting.

COLLAR
Corduroy for warmth and water repellency.

PLACKET
Covered to avoid buttons getting caught in the brush.

POCKETS
Provide utility and storage, including two-flapped, segmented pockets for storing shotgun cartridges.

Canvas hunting jacket. Photograph by Bill Steele

Backing Up

For as long as people have had something to carry, they've needed something to carry it in. In the past, animal hides were used in Europe, while in Asia, baskets with straps served the purpose. American children used to carry their schoolbooks bound together with a single leather strap. The modern backpack probably originated in the Alpine countries, where it was necessary to have both hands free for hiking through the mountains. In the first half of the 20th century, these rucksacks (from the German word for backpack) were considered quaint and rustic, but their basic design would serve as the pattern for today's most popular unisex bag. In the late sixties, when all things army-navy were in vogue, the olive army pack served as a carryall, while the rise of affordable European travel saw an increase in carrying all worldly goods in one giant bag, in the lifestyle we came to know as backpacking. The crossover from hiking gear to everyday wear began at the University of Washington, where students used camping day packs by JanSport to protect their books from Seattle's constant rainfall. By the early eighties, other day-pack and duffel-bag manufacturers, notably Eastpak, got in on the action, and high-end black leather versions of the backpack appeared. Backpacks with a bootlegged Louis Vuitton logo popped up in urban centers in the early nineties (the company released its own official version, the Montsouris, in 1996), as did high-tech nylon models by athletic companies like Adidas and Nike, surf companies like Quiksilver and O'Neill, luggage manufacturers like Tumi (which produces the popular Kipling line), and sportswear designers like Tommy Hilfiger, DKNY, and Polo Sport.

Flannel shirts are always appropriate for being outdoors in the city or the country. They can be worn as overshirts over a turtleneck or a henley, but they look the most authentic with corduroys or jeans and boots.

A Shirt for Everyman

The humble flannel shirt, a descendant of the wool CPO overshirt, was originally designed to keep hunters warm. Before the mid-sixties, they were largely worn for their intended purpose: outdoor activities. In the late sixties, their sturdy construction, low price, and blue-collar authenticity made them instant campus classics. In the seventies, gay men wore them as part of the macho-man wardrobe, often with the sleeves cut off. Worn around the waist by hard-core punk bands and their followers in the early eighties, the flannel shirt (and, later, shorts) became a staple of the Seattle-based grunge look. While most American sportswear manufacturers offer a version of the plaid flannel shirt, the signature brands are L. L. Bean, Woolrich, Pendleton, Eddie Bauer, Orvis, and Patagonia.

WHY BUFFALO?

A distinctively American look (not a Scottish tartan), buffalo shirts are so named because, in the 1850s, the man who created the oversized two-color checks (black with red, blue, white, yellow, or green) also raised buffalo.

EVERY FOURTH OF JULY, WE'D HAVE A **COOKOUT** AT MY AUNT MARIAN'S, WITH HER FIVE KIDS AND MY EIGHT BROTHERS AND SISTERS RUNNING AROUND, PLAYING SOFTBALL AND BADMINTON, EATING HOT DOGS WITH KETCHUP AND MUSTARD, POTATO SALAD, AND CHERRY PIE—THE AMERICAN FAVORITES.

Harvest time is value time on

Heinz
RED
MAGIC

THE WORLD'S LARGEST-SELLING   KETCHUP

FAMILY SIZE

HEINZ TOMATO KETCHUP
ESTD 1869
57 VARIETIES
HEINZ
MADE BY
H.J. HEINZ COMPANY

Look for
Heinz Ketchup
Chili Sauce
Hot Ketchup
—specially
featured at
your food
store

Heinz makes **everything** taste better!

57

DOING THE BARBECUE RIGHT hot dogs, hamburgers, chicken, shish kebob, mustard, ketchup, bread-and-butter pickles, chips and salsa, Ruffles potato chips and Lipton soup dip, corn on the cob, potato salad, baked beans, cole slaw, lemonade, Coca-Cola, beer, blender drinks, "s'mores," ice cream, Tiki torches, Hawaiian shirts, Bermuda shorts, chef's apron, chef's hat, Weber kettle grills, butterfly chairs, picnic tables

My mother wore a gingham dress, and my sisters wore blue gingham. Our tablecloths were red gingham. Even the western shirt on my back was red gingham.

Lucille Ball and Desi Arnaz in
The Long Long Trailer, 1954

THE GINGHAM SHIRT

Gingham (from the Malaysian GINGGANG, meaning checked cloth), in its most traditional form, is a woven pattern, a white ground with colored checks that measure 1/4 inch. Best known for the red and white tablecloths found in Italian restaurants, gingham has a homespun charm and is a popular fabric for home decoration as well as clothing. Famous gingham wearers include Raggedy Ann, film critic Rex Reed, Mary Anne (from Gilligan's Island), and hamburger-chain mascot Bob's Big Boy.

GAMES OF SIMPLE PLAY
Outdoor activities for the not necessarily athletic

Badminton

Capture the flag

Croquet

Dodge ball

Flag football

Hackysack

Hopscotch

Horseshoes

Lawn darts

Mother may I?

Rain on the roof

Red rover

Shuffleboard

Slip 'n' slide

Sprinkler tag

Tetherball

Touch football

Tug-of-war

Ultimate Frisbee

Volleyball

Frankie Lymon and the Teenagers, 1961

CLASSICS

When I was growing up, clothes intrigued me. They were a barometer of my self-esteem and my status at school.

Like most other teenagers, I was a fashion conformist. I wore chinos, five-pocket stretch jeans, Clarke's desert boots, button-down shirts, madras jackets, navy blazers, and crew-neck sweaters. Very Ivy League. As a teenager in the sixties, I was in on the first wave of army-navy fashion. The hippies were wearing military-surplus items because they were inexpensive and anti-establishment. It was a deliberately ironic statement for peace protesters to be turned out in army uniforms. The military greatcoat, a big navy blue wool coat with brass buttons, was one of my favorites. I also wore sailor's bell bottoms and midi shirts with a sailor collar, or a blue-and-white striped boat-neck sweater.

These days I like to keep things simple, especially when I get up in the morning with a lot on my mind. I exercise, read the papers, scrub up, give myself the marching orders for the day. I always wear a white or blue shirt. In the summer I

wear chinos, and in the winter, gray flannel trousers. On the weekends I usually wear casual athletic clothes, and at night I often wear darker colors—maybe a turtleneck or velvet jeans or a jacket. But I always dress preppy during the week—it's simple and easy—that's my uniform.

Sometimes I am a bit of a chameleon. Some days I feel like playing the rock-star role, or wearing a motorcycle jacket and a pair of jeans and boots. As a designer, I'm really into luxurious fabrics. I appreciate finely combed broadcloth shirts, pajamas, boxers, and cashmere socks, as well as cashmere blazers by Hermès and many items by Gucci or Prada. But just as much I like a pair of corduroys or a pair of beat-up army twill pants.

Clothes are costumes. Every day people put on what they want to be. They create their own reality. We never stop playing dress-up. As kids, we do it outlandishly to imitate our parents; as adults, we do it to please ourselves and others. If you wear a very serious business suit, that says one thing, and if you wear something baggy and logoed, or maybe straight and crisp, all tucked-in and preppy, it says another. And then there are those who can wear a suit all week and dress in drag on the weekend. Whatever.

Fashion is a language. I speak to people all the time through style, silhouette, attitude, and color. Color is emotion. I like blues, I like Day-Glos and neutral tones. I love the colors of nature: sand, water, trees, and sky. If I'm someplace sunny, I might choose pastels; for colder climates, I'll go with deeper, richer tones. I love the colors of jelly beans, sherbets, and licorice. I couldn't live without basic black.

Fashion is also an art—of making sure that the zippers work well, the wash and shade are right, and all the ingredients are exact. It's very much like cooking; you have to have the right blend of spices and salt and pepper. I don't believe in pretentious fashion, in clothes that are exorbitantly priced, unwearable, or created as artwork for a museum but never available or accessible on the street.

In my view, fashion is for the moment, but style is an enduring frame of mind. People with good taste never have to try too hard because they know that if you spend too much time looking in the mirror, you'll only end up confused, and they understand that confidence is the ultimate fashion accessory. Self-assured people can wear anything.

The key to style is comfort. Clothes should feel lived in, not just put on. If your clothes make you feel out of place, simplify. If you're not sure what to wear, there are a wealth of classic American styles that look good on everyone.

THE GREAT THING ABOUT **JEANS** IS THAT THEY LOOK RIGHT NO MATTER HOW YOU CHOOSE TO WEAR THEM. WHETHER BAGGY OR TIGHT, JEANS SHOULD LOOK LIKE THEY'VE BEEN YOURS FOR 100 YEARS.

I LIKE TO SEE JEANS WORN WITH A THICK, HEAVY-DUTY LEATHER BELT OR WEBBED FABRIC BELT, AS WORN IN THE MILITARY. THE BUCKLE SHOULD BE SOLID, LIKE DOUBLE D-RINGS OR OLD WESTERN BUCKLES. REMEMBER THE DOUBLE-PRONG BELT BUCKLE ON THE COVER OF THE ROLLING STONES' *STICKY FINGERS?* THAT WAS THE COOLEST.

Custom Jeans and Jeans Customs

Tough and independent, denim is more than just an American way of dressing; it's a billboard for individuality. For the past 50 years, denim has achieved an ever-changing uniqueness by being the canvas through which youth expresses itself.

In the fifties, purism reigned. The newer and bluer your jeans looked, the better. Rolled cuffs revealing the reverse weave of the fabric provided contrast.

Old denim became popular in the sixties. The frayed look was in. Colorful patchwork made jeans a living quilt, and triangular inserts were sewn into straight-legged jeans to transform them into groovy bell bottoms. Some folks even split their jeans at the leg seam, added grommets, and laced them back together.

In the seventies, flares were worn with flair. It was a sign of coolness to have the bottoms of your unhemmed jeans torn from walking on them. Gay men sandpapered the crotches of their jeans to make them more eye-catching. By the end of the decade, punk rockers safety-pinned the legs of their jeans for the tightest fit ever.

Designer jeans ruled the eighties—the tighter the better. People would wear their jeans in the tub and sit out in the sun to dry in order to achieve the perfect fit. Jeans were sold stone-washed, acid-washed, and overdyed in acid colors, but that still didn't stop people from bleaching, ripping, and shredding their jeans or from adding beads, jewels, and sequins.

In the nineties, purity is the trend. People like their jeans honest, whether they're faded relics or starched and dry-cleaned to preserve their color and shape.

Denim: The Rebel Kind

Dateline Anytown, U.S.A. "Alert! Scientists discover denim pants cause juvenile delinquency in teenagers!"

A decade of dishing out denim was kicked off in 1951 when Bing Crosby, America's favorite crooner, was refused a room in a Canadian hotel by a desk clerk who was not allowed to admit anyone into the high-toned resort wearing low-class denim.

In 1957 the venerable Levi Strauss company ran an ad depicting a clean-cut young boy wearing Levi's jeans with the slogan "right for our school." It attracted attention, all right—the wrong kind. One outraged parent wrote that perhaps wearing Levi's was right for school in the west, but not for Peoria. A move to ban Levi's as school wear was launched.

But to no avail. By the end of the fifties, Levi's jeans had become the rage of leisure-loving teenage boys and their older college-age brothers. Though the mere sight of a pair would cause conniption fits in most adults of the day, the majority of America's youth—90 percent according to a newspaper report—wore their blue denims everywhere except in bed and to church.

Jeans became the unisex uniform of the sixties Woodstock generation. Painted, patched, appliquéd, covered in leather and suede, they became the ultimate symbol of individuality and homegrown rebellion.

Andy Warhol made jeans go POP on the cover of the Rolling Stones' STICKY FINGERS album in 1971 by featuring a life-sized depiction of Joe Dallesandro's crotch. This was denim as erogenous zone, a precursor to the ultra-tight designer-jeans era of the late seventies. Throughout the seventies, denim was flared, belled, and turned into outfits of vests, pants, and matching "poor-boy" caps. Three-piece suits of chemically faded blue denim were added to the Levi's line, along with patchwork denim pants-and-vest combos.

The world was informed in a 1982 TV commercial that "nothing" came between Brooke Shields and her Calvins. From that moment on, nothing could be sold to the American public quicker than another pair of designer jeans. Designers such as Sergio Valente, Joujou, and Diane Von Furstenberg all made their mark, but by the end of the decade, Levi's were still the most popular and sought-after jeans worldwide.

The nineties brought denim shirts even into the office, jeans jackets refashioned in leather, satin, and corduroy, as well as jeans in every which way, including loose. It was the era of casual clothing, and the "relaxed fit" worked for everyone from aging baby boomers to hip-hop fans.

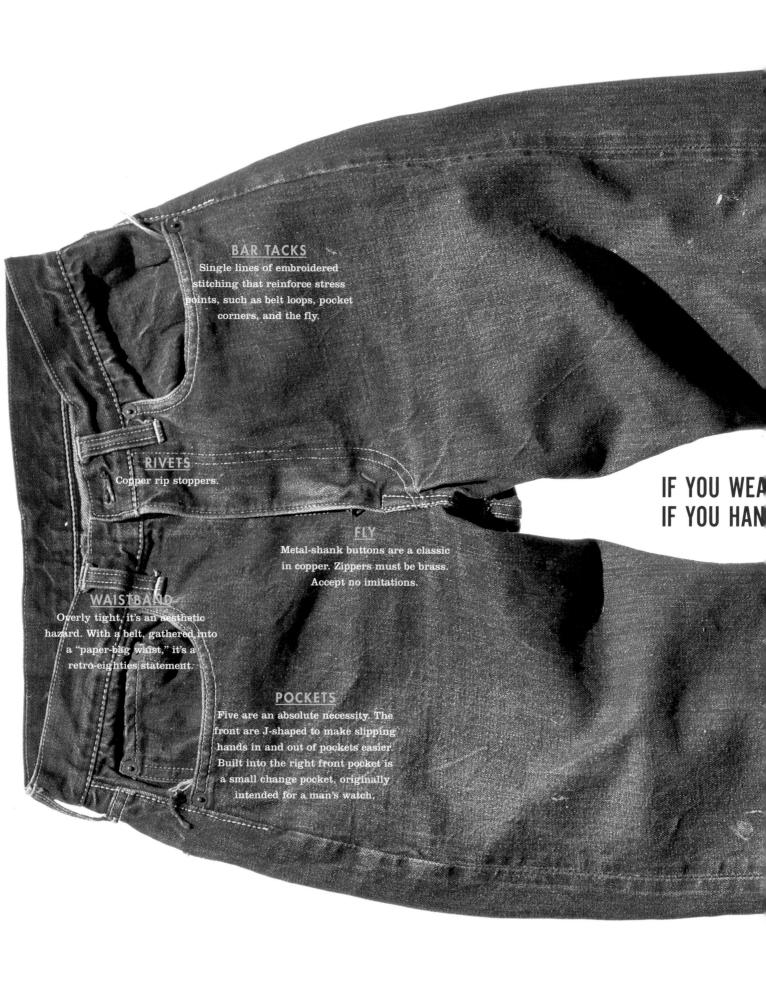

BAR TACKS
Single lines of embroidered
stitching that reinforce stress
points, such as belt loops, pocket
corners, and the fly.

RIVETS
Copper rip stoppers.

FLY
Metal-shank buttons are a classic
in copper. Zippers must be brass.
Accept no imitations.

WAISTBAND
Overly tight, it's an aesthetic
hazard. With a belt, gathered into
a "paper-bag waist," it's a
retro-eighties statement.

POCKETS
Five are an absolute necessity. The
front are J-shaped to make slipping
hands in and out of pockets easier.
Built into the right front pocket is
a small change pocket, originally
intended for a man's watch.

IF YOU WEA
IF YOU HAN

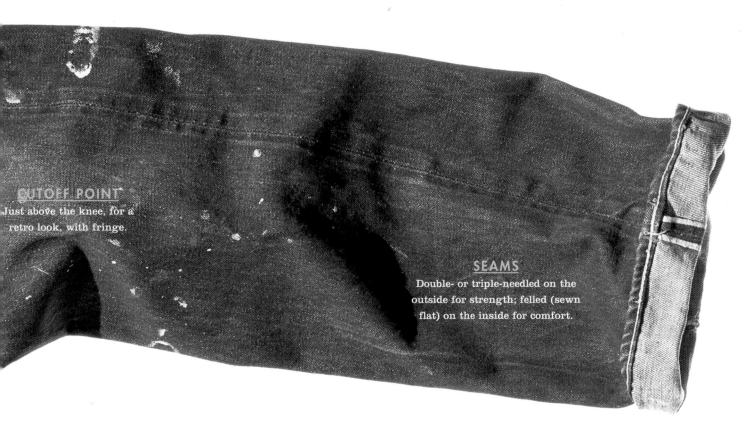

ANS TIGHT, HAVE A CLEAN DOUBLE-STITCHED HEM THAT COVERS YOUR ANKLES.
OSE, JUST ROLL THEM UP TWO AND A HALF INCHES.

Vintage Levi's (courtesy of Starstruck, New York). Photograph by Bill Steele

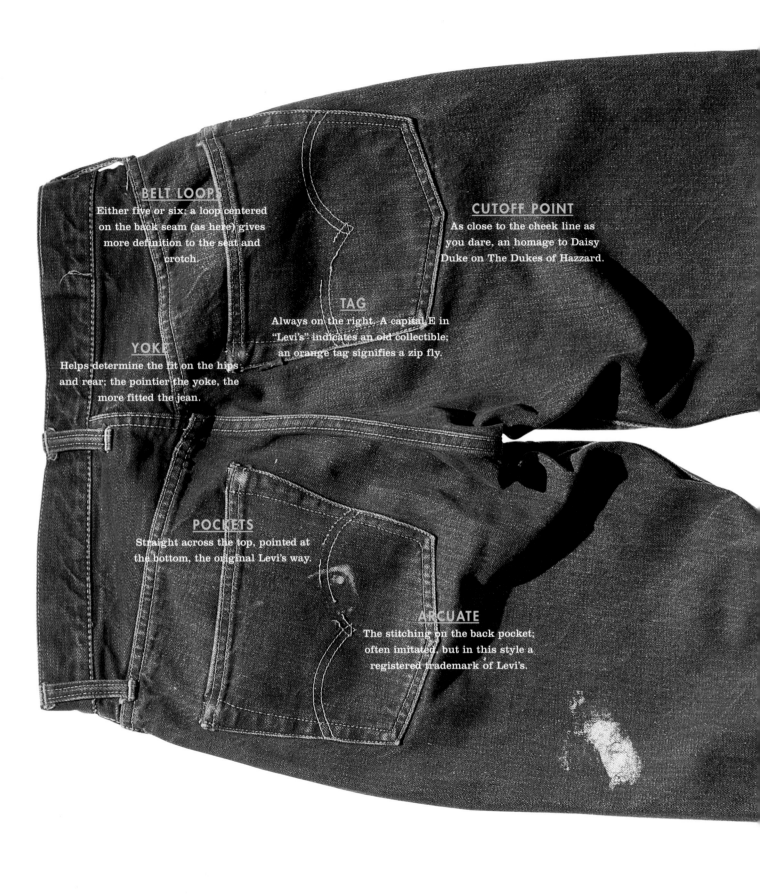

BELT LOOPS
Either five or six; a loop centered
on the back seam (as here) gives
more definition to the seat and
crotch.

CUTOFF POINT
As close to the cheek line as
you dare, an homage to Daisy
Duke on The Dukes of Hazzard.

TAG
Always on the right. A capital E in
"Levi's" indicates an old collectible;
an orange tag signifies a zip fly.

YOKE
Helps determine the fit on the hips
and rear; the pointier the yoke, the
more fitted the jean.

POCKETS
Straight across the top, pointed at
the bottom, the original Levi's way.

ARCUATE
The stitching on the back pocket;
often imitated, but in this style a
registered trademark of Levi's.

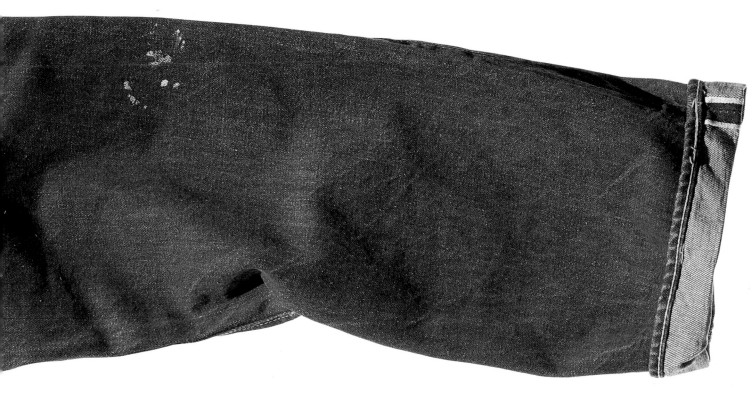

EANS SHOULD LOOK AND FEEL FADED AND COMFORTABLE, AND BE SOMEWHAT
RREVERENT, LIKE YOU DON'T HAVE A REGULAR JOB AND YOU DON'T CARE.

DENIM

Only 14.5-ounce indigo-dyed twill
will do. Sewn with size 604
"antique bronze" thread.

Vintage Levi's (courtesy of Starstruck, New York). Photograph by Bill Steele

The Big Three

LEVI STRAUSS & CO.

The patch on the back of the jeans says that the company was established on May 20, 1873, but the first pair of Levi's jeans was produced in 1872. In that year, Jacob Davis, a tailor in Reno, Nevada, wrote to Levi Strauss, who'd provided canvas and denim clothing for the gold-rush miners and who'd had a wholesale dry-goods business in San Francisco since 1853. Davis offered to come up with a way to rivet the corners of pockets and suggested they take out a patent on the process.

The copper-riveted jeans were known officially as "waist overalls" (and were until 1960); they had only one back pocket, a watch pocket, a cinch, and suspender buttons. In 1886 the leather patch that shows two horses trying vainly to pull the product apart was introduced onto the back of the pants. Around 1890, lot numbers were first employed, and the number 501 was assigned to the signature waist overalls. By 1900 there were two back pockets. Fast-forward to 1967, when lot number 501Z (Z for zipper) became 502-0117 and 501 was used exclusively for the button-fly.

501s are the original, classic, Shrink-to-Fit Levi's, the standard against which all other denim jeans are measured and compared. The Red Tab Device on the back pocket, indicating that the pants are the original, top-of-the-line product, was created in 1936 to identify 501s from a distance. Silver Tab is the Levi Strauss fashion line (with silverish tab and rivets) and comes in a spectrum of colors, including walnut brown, cardinal red, maize, stone, and copper.

The double-bow pattern stitched onto the back pockets of all Levi's is called the Arcuate Design and is the oldest clothing trademark still in use. The durable brown patch that is sewn onto the waistband and embossed with waist and inseam measurements was originally leather, then linen, and is now a special compound identified as "leatherlike—a special family recipe."

LEE APPAREL CO., INC.

Vermont-born Henry David Lee moved west to Ohio at age 13, saved $1,200 working for three years as a hotel clerk, invested in real estate and livery, and eventually purchased Central Oil Company. A sickly man, Lee was forced to sell his business to John D. Rockefeller's Standard Oil Company in 1886, and he relocated to Salina, Kansas, where he established the H. D. Lee Mercantile Company, a wholesale grocery business, and expanded into clothing. Unable to keep enough overalls and dungarees in stock due to unreliable deliveries from eastern suppliers, he decided to start building his own garment factories.

In 1913, Lee's chauffeur is rumored to have come up with an idea. He suggested that the firm develop a one-piece work-wear garment that could be slipped on over his chauffeur's uniform, for when he was underneath the automobile or changing a tire, but that would also serve as an ideal outfit for farm and factory workers wanting to keep debris from getting between their clothes and their skin. Lee employees sewed a jacket and a pair of dungarees together, and the Lee Union-All was born.

The Union-All became the U.S. Army's official doughboy fatigue during World War I. The twenties saw Lee making railroad uniforms and cowboy outfits, and introducing the "denim cowboy pant." In 1926, Lee introduced "buttonless" jeans with zippers, work clothes with slide fasteners, and the U-shaped saddle crotch and tailored sizing, in which rise and seat proportions were based on waist and inseam measurements. Lee went on to outfit James Arness in Gunsmoke, the cast of The Beverly Hillbillies, and Hollywood's Ronald Reagan. In 1964, Lee introduced "no-iron" permanent-press slacks under its Lee Prest label. In 1972, Lee introduced the leisure suit, "a sporty interpretation of the business suit," followed a year later by Ms. Lee, a new label for women.

WRANGLER, INC.

"Real cowboys don't wear Levi's" is a kind of mantra in Greensboro, North Carolina, where the original Wrangler western-wear product, the 13MWZ, was designed and manufactured in 1947. So it is fitting that 12,000 pairs of cowboy-cut jeans and other Wrangler products were ordered by Robert Redford for the cast of THE HORSE WHISPERER, filmed in New York and Montana in 1997. The code 13MWZ stands for the 13th prototype of the Men's Western Zipper style—cowboys call 'em "13s."

Ben Liechtenstein, a.k.a. "Rodeo Ben," a Philadelphia tailor, who specialized in making outfits for rodeo performers and cowboy-movie stars like Roy Rogers and Gene Autry, was the designer of the first Wrangler western jeans. To research what men needed in the jeans they wore on the trail or at home on the range, Ben traveled west and canvassed a posse of cowpokes. Their advice: (1) More belt loops to accommodate wide leather belts with big buckles. A mere five loops had been the standard. (2) Rear pockets higher up so the buckaroos wouldn't have to sit on the lumps made by their wallets while in the saddle. (3) Smooth rivets around the pockets that wouldn't scratch their beloved saddles. (4) A watch pocket snug enough to prevent loss of watches and coins. (5) A long inseam so the jeans wouldn't ride up to the top of the boot when sitting tall in the saddle. (6) A heavy-duty zipper, maneuverable while wearing riding gloves. Prior to this, buttons had been standard issue.

So Rodeo Ben went to work filling this tall order. When finished, he capped off his sartorial achievement by designing a patch for the back of the jeans, with the name Wrangler scripted in a rope motif. The patch was made of Neolite, a sturdy material used in shoe soles, which, unlike leather, didn't shrink and wrinkle when washed. Today the patch graces the backsides of over 98 percent of the Professional Rodeo Cowboys Association membership.

Denim shirts and jackets say traditional
American work wear, but at the same time
they have a relaxed, Saturday flavor.
The acceptance of the jeans shirt as a
casual alternative for the office is proof
that, in today's world, denim has become
an established way of life.

Steve McQueen

ORIGINAL DENIM
The word "denim" derives from
SERGE DE NIMES, Nimes being the city
in southern France where the soft, durable
fabric was invented in the 1500s. Levi Strauss
imported the material from Nimes in 1873
and added a twist by dyeing it indigo. The
classic Levi's jacket has no side pockets.

Jackson Pollock. Photograph by Hans Namuth, 1952

I COULDN'T WEAR A **T-SHIRT** TO SCHOOL. I REMEMBER IN 1969 I WORE A DYED-PURPLE WALLACE BEERY HENLEY, ONE OF THOSE OLD-FASHIONED UNDERSHIRTS, TO SCHOOL ONCE. THEY TOOK ONE LOOK AT ME AND SAID, "YOU'VE GOT AN UNDERSHIRT ON. GO HOME."

Paul Newman at the Actors Studio. Photograph by Eve Arnold, 1955

Paul Newman in Hud, 1963

Photograph by Cornell Capa, 1958

There was a time when wearing a T-shirt was a rebellious statement, a way of saying you were a no-nonsense, hardworking guy. Today it is every bit as athletic and sexy, but also the height of casual style.

T-Times

In the beginning, T-shirts were meant to be worn loosely underneath shirts to keep you warm and keep them dry. For those who didn't want the top of the T-shirt to show underneath an unbuttoned collar (a look that has become a preppy staple), there were V-necks and sleeveless undershirts. Once the T-shirt became acceptable outerwear, its size, shape, cut, and decoration became a reliable badge of the wearer's identity. The greasers were the first to adopt the tight white T-shirt as a uniform, usually with a pack of filterless smokes rolled up in one sleeve. Sans cigarettes, the tight white T-shirt has been a macho symbol for men of every lifestyle and sexual orientation.

In the sixties, T-shirts took on color: bright horizontal stripes on baggy shirts for surfers, rainbow-colored tie-dyed and batik shirts for hippies (and now Deadheads and hackysack players). In the seventies, T-shirts shrank.

Sleeves were capped at the shoulder (often with a colored hem), and hems cropped to midriff length; decorations often included big silver stars and words spelled out in metallic studs.

In the new-wave era, the T-shirt went XXL. British designer Katharine Hamnett scored big with oversized messages on oversized T-shirts (popularized by the pop group Frankie Goes to Hollywood), and some girls wore belted huge T-shirts as dresses. In the nineties, there is something for everyone: body-fitting T-shirts in stretchy, sheer, and luxury fabrics for the athletic and high-fashion types, extra-roomy T-shirts with logos and futuristic graphics that fit hip-hop kids and the rave generation, even T-shirts under button-down shirts—like on the guys in the television show Friends.

Tony Curtis

WHEN I WAS YOUNG, BOXER SHORTS WERE FOR OLD MEN. FOR JUST ABOUT EVERYONE ELSE,

UNDERWEAR

CAME IN ONE COLOR AND STYLE. TIGHTY WHITIES. NOWADAYS, THERE ARE SO MANY OPTIONS. BOXERS LOOK GOOD ON EVERYONE, ESPECIALLY IF YOU HAVE A BELLY. IF YOU'RE THIN, BRIEFS LOOK GOOD; FOR THE MID-THIGH STYLE, YOU SHOULD BE FIT SINCE IT DRAWS ATTENTION TO THE LEGS; FOR A BIKINI, YOU HAVE TO BE IN INCREDIBLE SHAPE; AND FOR A THONG, YOU HAVE TO BE A MODEL IN A GUCCI AD.

Jockey advertisements, 1953

Underwear:
A Brief History

Tom Cruise in Risky
Business, *1983*

1934 is a year to remember: that year, in IT HAPPENED ONE NIGHT, Clark Gable took off his shirt to reveal a bare chest, and the market for undershirts took a bath. That was also the year an executive from Jockey International, Inc., inspired by a postcard of a bikini-clad man on the Riviera, redesigned men's knit underwear. The following year, Jockey International introduced the Y-front brief (a configuration of fabric panels and seams that make up the buttonless fly opening). Soldiers wore newfangled army-issue briefs in World War II, and thereafter, once they returned home, they preferred their briefs.

For a while, briefs separated the boys from the men. In the nineties, bikini cuts (said to offer the greatest enhancement of God's gifts to you) created another generation gap.

In the late eighties, everything got mixed up: guys started wearing colorful boxer shorts to hang out in or hit the beach (and girls liked them for the same reasons), or sticking out from under a pair of baggy jeans. The fitness movement, particularly the craze for bike shorts, led to elongated briefs (which fit better than boxers under jeans and lean trousers) and even unitards. And for the fearless or flawlessly shaped, the thong arrived from Brazil.

(Y-front is a trademark of and used with permission of Jockey International, Inc.)

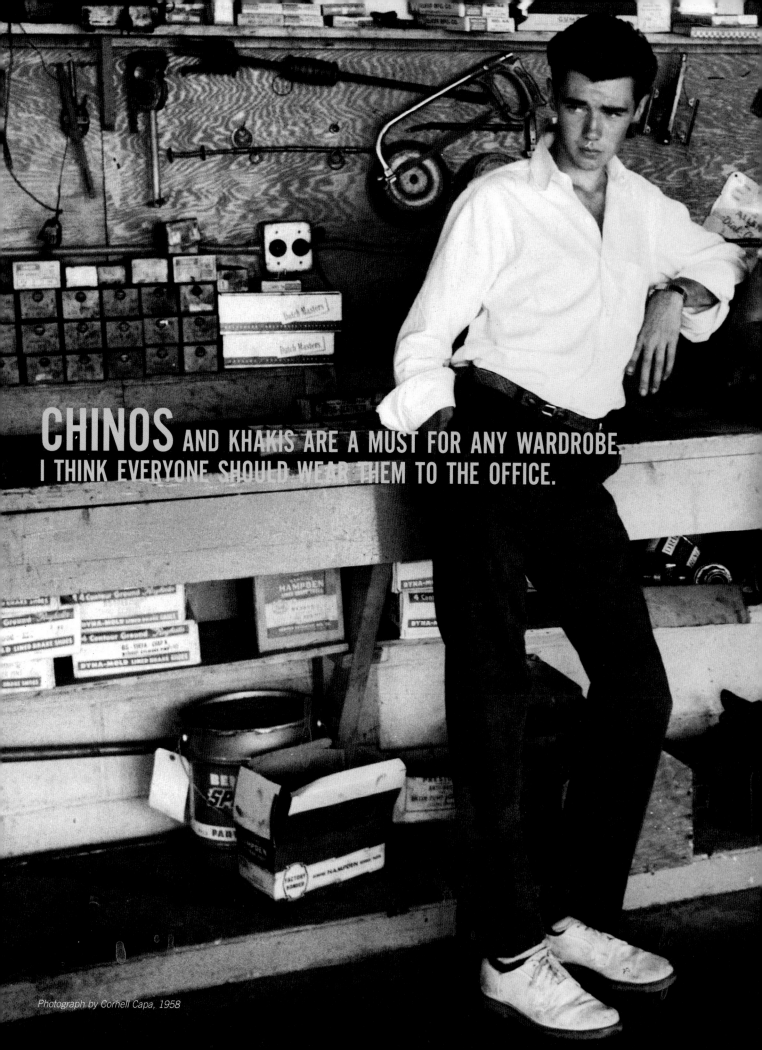

CHINOS AND KHAKIS ARE A MUST FOR ANY WARDROBE. I THINK EVERYONE SHOULD WEAR THEM TO THE OFFICE.

Photograph by Cornell Capa, 1958

THE KHAKI DRILL

Khakis come from the Urdu word KHAK, which means dust or earth. Originally they were the warm-weather military trousers worn by the English. They picked up their nickname, chinos, because, until American sportswear manufacturers began making them, they were largely made in China.

These days, there are a lot of styles of chinos. You can wear them with short hems, like they used to do in the sixties, when preppies called them highwaters or floods, or you can wear them loose and baggy, like they do today on Cape Cod. You can toss them in the washing machine and then throw them on or send them to the dry cleaners and get them back with a sharp crease down the leg. They look good with a T-shirt, blazer, or black cashmere sweater.

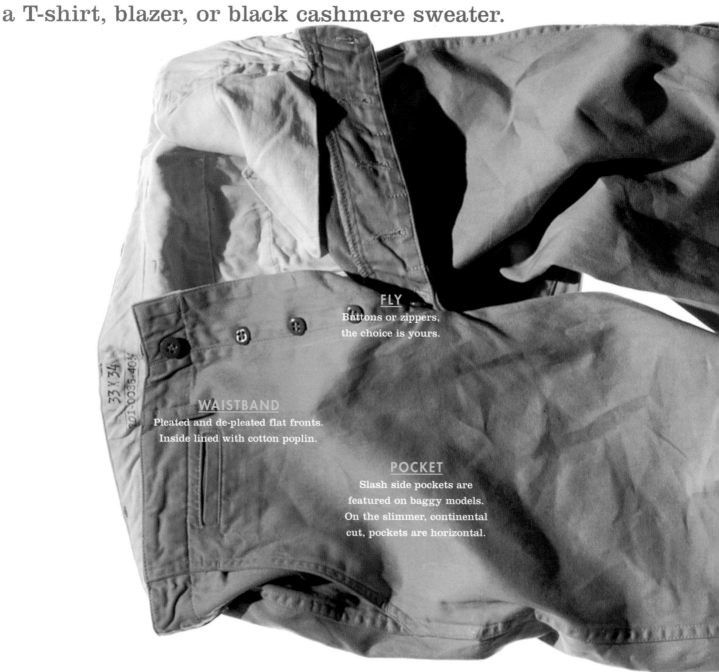

FLY
Buttons or zippers, the choice is yours.

WAISTBAND
Pleated and de-pleated flat fronts.
Inside lined with cotton poplin.

POCKET
Slash side pockets are featured on baggy models.
On the slimmer, continental cut, pockets are horizontal.

FABRIC
Army-issue khakis are heavier than chinos in cotton twill; newer styles are more formfitting with stretch fabrics.

Fifties chinos (courtesy of Fools and Horses, Brooklyn, New York). Photograph by Bill Steele

I DIDN'T GO TO COLLEGE; I WAS LEARNING A LOT ANYWAY BY RUNNING MY OWN BUSINESS. BUT I LIVED NEAR CORNELL, ITHACA, COLGATE, HAMILTON, AND AN ALL-WOMEN'S SCHOOL IN ELMIRA, AND WE USED TO DRIVE TO THE CAMPUSES AND HANG OUT. THERE WERE PARTIES, CONCERTS, SPORTS, DANCES—ALL THESE KIDS JUST HAVING FUN. AND THE WAY EVERYBODY DRESSED WAS IRREVERENT

IVY LEAGUE.

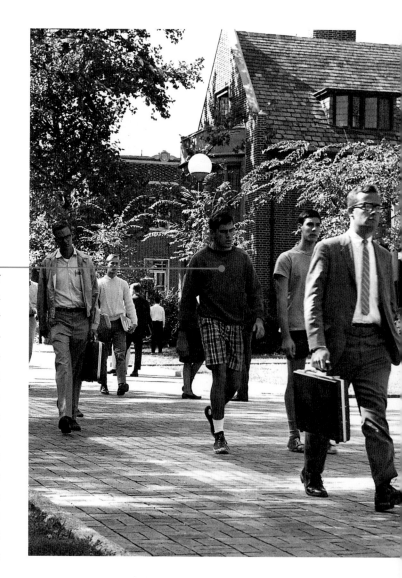

Sweating It Out

In the beginning, college athletes wore wool sweaters during competition, usually with the letter of their school appliquéd in felt on the front; later the letters were interwoven. (The letter sweater, which became popular after World War II as a cardigan, was more for show than for play.) In the twenties, the Knickerbocker Knitting Company, the first company to sell sweatshirts with academic logos (the first being Wentworth Military Academy in Lexington, Kentucky), changed its name to Champion because so much of the business was with the university sports teams. From 1919 to 1938, logoed, fleeced cotton sweatshirts were used for warm-up practices. Responding to complaints from athletes that the all-cotton sweatshirt shrank in the wash, Champion employee Sam Friedland patented the reverse-weave process in 1938. In the late eighties, the hooded sweatshirt became a universal fashion statement, whether worn by suburban sports fans, hip-hop kids, or gay activists.

Polo coats

Stadium boxy blazers

Tweed jackets with suede elbow patches

Navy blazers with crests

Madras shirts

Flannel shirts

Oxford shirts

Rep striped ties

Crew-neck sweaters

Cardigans and letter sweaters

Argyle sweaters

Sweater vests

Corduroys

Khakis

Gray flannel slacks

White socks

Argyle socks

Penny loafers

Flat caps

Wing tips

NOW

Down jackets

Hooded sweatshirts

Jeans

Chinos

Track pants

V-neck sweaters

Vintage sports jackets

Plaid flannel shirts

Jams

Cargo pants

Carpenter pants

Camouflage pants

Anoraks

University T-shirts and sweats

Doc Martens

Birkenstocks

Running shoes

Baseball caps

Photograph by Elliott Erwitt

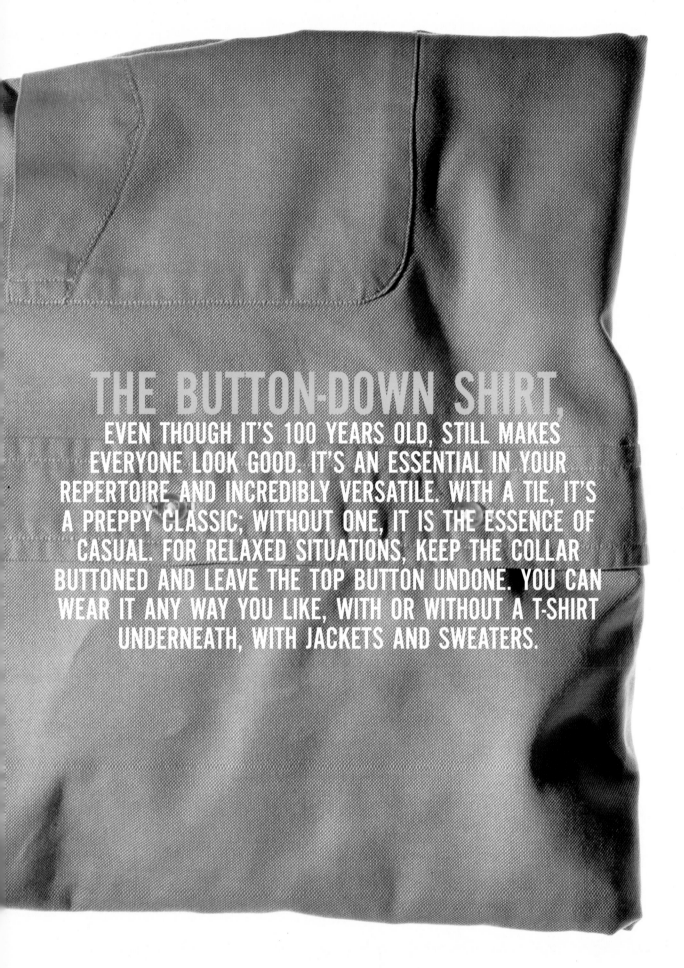

THE BUTTON-DOWN SHIRT,

EVEN THOUGH IT'S 100 YEARS OLD, STILL MAKES EVERYONE LOOK GOOD. IT'S AN ESSENTIAL IN YOUR REPERTOIRE AND INCREDIBLY VERSATILE. WITH A TIE, IT'S A PREPPY CLASSIC; WITHOUT ONE, IT IS THE ESSENCE OF CASUAL. FOR RELAXED SITUATIONS, KEEP THE COLLAR BUTTONED AND LEAVE THE TOP BUTTON UNDONE. YOU CAN WEAR IT ANY WAY YOU LIKE, WITH OR WITHOUT A T-SHIRT UNDERNEATH, WITH JACKETS AND SWEATERS.

Sixties button-down shirt. Photograph by Bill Steele

HOW TO BUY
A COTTON SHIRT

All shirts are not created equal. For the finest quality, feel the fabric. Egyptian and Sea Island cottons have the smoothest surface, with a high thread count (the number of threads per square inch). Pima cotton, introduced in 1925, is an exceptionally strong and firm hybrid of Egyptian cottons developed in Pima County, Arizona. Most shirts, however, are made from oxford cloth, a soft, durable cotton that takes starch like nobody's business, in a plain or basket weave (the latter is most typically found on button-down shirts), or broadcloth, a soft, somewhat glossy cotton that tends to wrinkle easily. For the coolest summer cotton, try end-on-end, a loose, breathable weave in which colored threads are interwoven with white, lending a subtle iridescence.

WHY BUTTON DOWN?

The button-down shirt was originally designed to keep collars from flapping into the faces of polo players as they rode at high speed across the field.

Anthony Perkins

All About Collars

The tab collar is mod and meticulous, with a fabric that buttons or snaps underneath a tie, pushing the knot (which should be small) front and center. The tab fits any face and is extremely flattering to heavier-set jawlines.

The round or club collar, a favorite of British schoolboys, has no points, and has holes for a tie bar which serve the same function as a tab collar.

The button-down was created by Brooks Brothers in 1900 and suits a wide variety of faces, with collars generally measuring between 3 1/8 to 3 1/4 inches long.

The straight or turndown collar varies in length according to the styles of the time, and is the most versatile, elongating short or round faces.

The wing collar is found on a formal shirt. Worn with tuxedos, it gives any face an air of elegance.

The spread collar requires a large tie knot and adds weight to a thin or finely featured face. It is not recommended for the jowly.

The contrast collar sets off a colored or patterned shirt with a pristine white collar. It's an eighties yuppie classic, adopted by CEOs, lawyers, investment bankers, and people with British tailors.

Tab Hunter

P4231-4

DEPENDING ON HOW YOU WEAR THEM, SWEATERS CAN MAKE YOU FEEL SOPHISTICATED AND SHARP OR COMFORTABLE AND COZY.

Pure Cashmere

The wool comes from the cashmere goat, which lives in Mongolia. It takes 16 goats to supply enough fiber to make a plush four-ply sweater.

Scottish cashmere is the finest in the world. Look for the Ballantyne, Scotch House, and Pringle labels.

Unlike mohair and angora, cashmere doesn't shed and is nearly wrinkle-proof. Cashmere blended with wool, nylon, and silk lends durability to hard-wearing garments like trousers and socks. Properly cared for, cashmere has a life span of 20 years.

Warren Beatty

Cardigan

Fisherman's sweater

Crew-neck Shetland

Ribbed turtleneck

Knit waistcoat

Varsity sweater

Letter sweater

Shawl-collar pullover

Suede-front cardigan

Scoop-neck poor-boy

Belted Guatemalan sweater

Punk mohair sweater

Long-sleeve polo sweater

Navajo sweater

Icelandic ski sweater

Lamb's-wool V-necks

Nautical sweaters (navy and
    white stripes or solid navy
    with buttons on the shoulder)

Argyle sweater vests

Ski sweaters

Fair Isles sweaters

Striped racing sweaters

Cashmere sweaters

Mister Rogers

HAND-SEWN IN NEW ENGLAND, **WEEJUNS** ARE THE OLD IVY LEAGUE CLASSICS. LIKE MOCCASINS, YOU CAN WEAR THEM WITH ANYTHING. YOU CAN WEAR THEM WITHOUT SOCKS, AND THE MORE BEAT UP THEY GET, THE BETTER THEY LOOK.

WHY A PENNY?

G. H. Bass & Co. introduced loafers in the U.S.
in the thirties, based on a design for Norwegian
peasant shoes, hence the nickname "Weejuns." They
were an instant hit for loafing around (therefore
becoming known as "loafers") on college campuses.
They had a leather "saddle" across the front, which
some bright fellow discovered could hold a penny,
which brings us to the familiar name
"penny loafers." Over the years,
this casual shoe has been streamlined and
refashioned in everything from shiny vinyl to red
suede, but the original—cordovan leather with beefy,
rolled stitching connecting the apron to each side
of the shoe—is still the greatest.

Fifties loafers. Photograph by Bill Steele

NO ONE LIKES TO
BE LABELED,
BUT YOU CAN TELL
A GOOD DEAL
ABOUT PEOPLE
BY THE
LABELS
THEY CHOOSE
TO WEAR
AND HOW THEY
WEAR THEM:
ON THE
SLEEVE
OR CLOSE
TO THE
CHEST.

Vintage labels. Thomas Oatman Collection

Closet Classics
The elements of the civil wardrobe

High tops
Loafers, sneakers, wing tips
Tank tops
Chesterfield coat
Leather gloves, mittens
Bomber jacket
Cotton socks and wool socks
Wool, cotton, cashmere, and
    fisherman's knit sweaters
Cargo pants
Anorak
Chinos, jeans, gray flannel and
    gray tropical-wool trousers
Carpenter pants
Western shirts
Tartan and regimental scarves
Barbour jacket
Stadium coat
Ski jacket, ski pants
Cardigans
Tuxedo
Jeans jacket
Pin-stripe, herringbone, solid
    gray or navy suit
Military shirts
Tennis gear, white
Ray-Ban aviators and Wayfarers
Ribbed turtleneck
Double D-ring, double-prong, and
    webbed belts
Golf sweater, pants, and shirts
Hawaiian shirts
Boxers and briefs
Button-down and tab-collar shirts
Wellies
Black grosgrain tie, black socks,
    and patent-leather shoes
Baseball cap, ski caps
Flannel, denim, corduroy, and
    chambray shirts
Sandals
Doc Martens
Military jacket
Riding pants and boots
Camel double-breasted polo coat
Rep striped tie
Peacoat
Bowling shirts
Topsiders
Basketball shorts
Jams
Square-cut bathing suit
Speedos

ANYTHING HAVING TO DO WITH **NAVY** IS AN EMOTIONAL TURN-ON. IT IS MY FAVORITE COLOR. I LOVE AIRCRAFT CARRIERS, SAILORS LINED UP, AND AMERICAN FLAGS BILLOWING IN THE WIND. I LOVE THE UNIFORMS OF NAVAL OFFICERS AND SWABBIES, THEIR STURDY CONSTRUCTION, CRISP FABRICS, AND ARCHITECTURAL SHAPES.

SAIL ON
Presenting sea legs and arms

Peacoats with anchor buttons

Chambray deck shirts

Square-collared midi top

Navy wool bell bottoms with 13 buttons

Navy-and-white striped boat-neck sweaters

Slickers

White cotton deck pants with two slit pockets

Fabric belts

Sailors in high wind. Photograph by Wayne Miller

SAILOR PANTS

The original navy sailor pants laced up in the back and had 13 decorative buttons in the front, representing the original colonies of the United States. The back-lacing trousers made for a tight fit, which helped sailors climb around the ship and kept them from getting caught up in the rigging. The famous bell bottom hem of sailor pants was designed to make rolling up the pants easier for those who were assigned to swab the deck.

PEOPLE LOVE GREAT QUALITY,
THEY LOVE RUGGEDNESS AND
A GREAT SOLID DESIGN. THAT'S
WHY FASHION DESIGNERS
CONTINUE TO PRODUCE FASHION
STATEMENTS FROM BASIC
SERVICE UNIFORMS FROM ALL
BRANCHES OF
THE MILITARY.
A LOT OF DETAIL HAS GONE
INTO THE MAKING OF THOSE
ITEMS: DOUBLE-STITCH SEAMS,
REINFORCED BAR TACKS, DEEP
REINFORCED POCKETS, HEAVY-
DUTY TWILLS MADE TO
WITHSTAND THE WEAR AND
TEAR OF SERVICE. AND
MILITARY UNIFORMS ARE
LIKE GREAT WINES—THEY
GET BETTER WITH AGE.

Private Elvis Presley, Fort Chaffee, Arkansas

G.I. BLUES AND KHAKIS

The best things in store at
the surplus outlet

Green army shoulder bags

Olive drab and camouflage T-shirts

Union suits

Flak jackets

Bundeswehr tank tops

Officer shirts

Flight suits

Flat-front khakis

Bomber jackets

Eisenhower jackets

Webbed belts

Camouflage pants and shirts

Berets

Waders and combat boots

Commando sweaters
    (with reinforced shoulders)

Drill trousers

Aviator shades

Pocketknives and canteens

Elvis Presley in G.I. Blues, *1960*

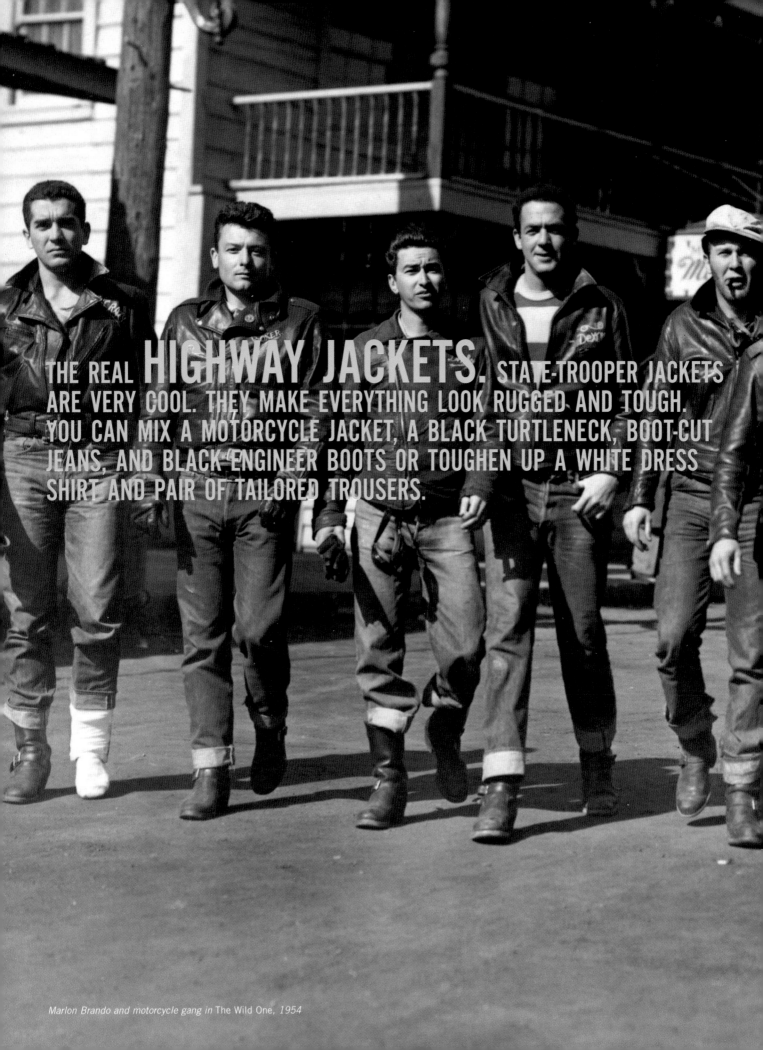

THE REAL **HIGHWAY JACKETS.** STATE-TROOPER JACKETS ARE VERY COOL. THEY MAKE EVERYTHING LOOK RUGGED AND TOUGH. YOU CAN MIX A MOTORCYCLE JACKET, A BLACK TURTLENECK, BOOT-CUT JEANS, AND BLACK ENGINEER BOOTS OR TOUGHEN UP A WHITE DRESS SHIRT AND PAIR OF TAILORED TROUSERS.

Marlon Brando and motorcycle gang in The Wild One, *1954*

THE PERFECTO

Irving Schott devised the leather motorcycle jacket in 1928, three years after he revolutionized outdoor sportswear by introducing the zipper into his jackets. Beginning in 1915, Schott's jackets were given the name Perfecto, after his favorite cigar. The Perfecto motorcycle jacket is worn for protection against both injury and the elements. It was a Harley-Davidson distributor who first approached Schott and suggested his jackets be used aboard motorcycles. In 1954, the Perfecto motorcycle jacket was featured in THE WILD ONE.

The Bomber Jacket

A war jacket for more peaceful times

In 1930, Irving Schott designed a leather jacket that he sold to the U.S. Air Force during World War II. The short jacket with deep pockets and epaulets was popular for its resilience and warmth among fighter pilots on bombing missions, hence the name "bomber jacket." The epaulets served as a handy place to stash glasses or a soft hat while flying.

Today the jacket is also known as the "flyer jacket." It comes in nylon as well as leather, and often features a quilted lining. The short style looks great with a pair of jeans. While the nylon version is versatile, nothing beats the feel of a vintage leather bomber jacket.

Vintage A-240 airman's jacket. Photograph by Bill Steele

HOW TO SHOP FOR A
VINTAGE LEATHER JACKET

Motorcycle jackets are the all-time favorite leather jackets. The most popular vintage ones are from the fifties—very old Schott, early Harley, and the Brand labels. But when looking for a vintage leather jacket, remember that a motorcycle jacket is not your only option. Bomber jackets, the real ones from World War II, are very durable and still available, some even with their original mink collars. Some actually have the original owner's airplane name inked onto the sleeve, which increases the jacket's worth. Note: Real bomber jackets are always brown. Always.

The feel of leather is as important as its appearance. Ideally, the best vintage motorcycle jackets are soft and fairly lightweight. When examining an old leather jacket, look for peeling or signs of dryness. You'll recognize the problem the moment you touch it. The earliest motorcycle jackets often featured wombat-fur lining. Today linings of older jackets are usually pretty beat up, but that is no gauge of the jacket's real worth. You can always replace the lining with a cotton-blend material made for that purpose.

It's usually pretty easy to tell if you are buying a real bomber jacket—look for an airforce insignia where the zipper is sewn in at the inside bottom of the jacket. One clue in sizing up a motorcycle jacket is that the more collectible ones from the forties and fifties never have as many zippers as jackets from the sixties.

THE MINUTE A MAN PUTS ON A **SUIT**, THERE'S A CHANGE IN HIS BEHAVIOR. IT'S THE BUSINESSMAN'S UNIFORM, HIS COAT OF ARMOR. THE STYLE, THE CUT, THE FABRIC, AND THE FIT ARE THE SIGNIFIERS OF HIS RANK AND INDIVIDUALITY.

The Man in the Gray Flannel Suit

Gregory Peck in The Man in the Gray Flannel Suit, *1967*

1940s

GANGSTERS AND HEROES

Although that extreme exaggeration of a suit, the Zoot, was popularized by bandleader Cab Calloway and worn with menacing enthusiasm by the "hep" and gangster crowds of the day, its street life was extremely brief. In 1942, three years after its introduction (allegedly inspired by the dress-up taste of Al Capp's cartoon character Li'l Abner), it was outlawed in the U.S. due to its flagrantly excessive use of cloth during wartime rationing. The War Production Board also saw to it that such wasteful details as cuffs, patch pockets, pleats, yokes, full or double anything, and vests were eliminated from men's suits in general. Finally, at war's (and wit's) end, the look we associate with the forties reared its rugged head—the hard silhouette of the full-cut double-breasted suit. Shoulders were padded, jacket buttons set lower, and lapels cut longer to accentuate height. The look was tall and slim, to be worn with spread-collar shirts and wide, Windsor-knotted ties. Gary Cooper, Cary Grant, and Clark Kent were the guys to reckon with. Recommended for the broad-shouldered or those who like to look it.

1950s

LEAN AND MODERN

The sack suit, popularized by Brooks Brothers and J. Press, blew into town with the Cold War. Nondescript, formless, and forgiving, it was natural-shouldered, with a thin silhouette—worn with thin lapels, thin tie, button-down shirt. It was part of conscripting the trim, conservative, conformist salary man into the daily work-force sea of olive drab and charcoal gray. Ivy League. Madison Avenue. Rock Hudson. Tony Randall. The Button-Down Mind of Bob Newhart. Gregory Peck in THE MAN IN THE GRAY FLANNEL SUIT, and of course the young JFK and RFK. For those who appreciate the sleek, slim, and slenderizing.

1960s

MODS AND CONTINENTALS

The skinny, shiny, center-vented version the sack suit, worn by the Rat Pack early the decade, evolved into the Continental lo from the pioneering menswear designe Pierre Cardin and Yves Saint Laurent. T tight-fitting suit featured strong padd shoulders, movement-restricting high armholes, and a nipped-in waist. The jack was side-vented and the trousers we tapered and cuffless. (By the end of t decade, the pants began to flare slightl Johnny Carson epitomized the Continent look, which later evolved further into t Edwardian dandy/mod/Carnaby Street sty that came over with the British music inv sion. A look for a decade of overpowerin variety.

Cary Grant

Rock Hudson

Dean Martin

1970s

OLYESTER LEISURE

ull-blown Continental. Wide lapels. 747
nirt collars. Represented by Roger Moore
s 007, it was a kind of modified safari suit
gabardine, featuring a fitted jacket with
apped chest pockets, and wide-flare bell
ottoms. Worn with long-pointed collar
irt, open at the neck. John Travolta, Peter
onda, Peter Sellers. Although it brought us
e polyester leisure suit, the decade also
w menswear designers finally get some
spect, most notably those who created an
nglo-American look by combining English
untry dressing with Hollywood glamour.
indulge, it helps to be rail thin, synthet-
-friendly, and aesthetically liberal.

1980s

DESIGNER TAILORING

A return to the elegance of the thirties and
forties—with a slouchy, unconstructed
Italian attitude. Kevin Costner and co-stars
arresting in Giorgio Armani in THE
UNTOUCHABLES. Richard Gere filing and
cross-referencing his G.A. in A.G. (Giorgio
Armani in AMERICAN GIGOLO). A little stiffer
was Michael Douglas wearing Allan Flusser
in WALL STREET—even the shirts seemed to
have shoulder pads. And then came the
Japanese garçons in the form of Comme des
Garçons and Yohji Yamamoto; it was like
going from Armani to origami. Dark,
sophisticated suits for nighttime; some were
so complicated in construction that they
really needed operating instructions. A
decade of classics and oddities, all worth a
second look.

1990s

REDEFINED ELEGANCE

Take your choice: one button, two, three,
four, or six buttons. With an eye for detail
and classic construction, suits shaped up. In
the early part of the decade, the theatrical
ruled: long, high-buttoned frock coats
teamed up with flat-front trousers for a
dandy look. Tuxedo dressing took a rock-
star turn, pairing dinner jackets with
leather pants and poetic shirts (sans tie). By
the end of the decade, classic Savile Row tai-
loring was updated for a new generation,
and a sleek new silhouette emerged, based
on the streamlined look of the early sixties,
with emphasis on clean lines and lustrous
fabrics, to be worn with solid-colored shirts
and ties.

John Travolta

Richard Gere

John Faureau and Vince Vaughn

THE APPEAL OF AMERICAN WORK CLOTHES
IS THE UTILITARIAN THOUGHT BEHIND THEM.
THEY'RE INEXPENSIVE, FUNCTIONAL, TOUGH,
AND DURABLE, AND YOU DON'T HAVE TO
IRON THEM. KHAKI OR FOREST GREEN PANTS
WORN WITH A WORK SHIRT CREATE A REALLY
CLEAN AND CRISP IMPRESSION. A

SERVICE-STATION

ATTENDANT WEARING NAVY PANTS
AND A LIGHT-BLUE SHIRT STITCHED WITH HIS
NAME CONVEYS AN HONEST MASCULINITY.

Working at the Hess station in Elmira, I had a shirt with
a big logo on the back. To me, it meant I was capable
of performing this grown-up duty in life. As long as
I can remember, wearing logos has been an
essential American style. People are proud to wear a name
that associates them with an organization. In fact, it
can help separate them from the crowd, giving
them a sense of security and authority.

Vintage garage-mechanic's uniform. Photograph by Bill Steele

COUGAR

OMET SAVE

EASY SELF SERV

DIXIE

GETMOR GAS

SAVE WITH DEAL GASOLINE

Old Dutch

BE SURE PURE WITH PURE

SHELL

SKELLY

STANDARD

Zephyr

The STINKE CUT RATE GAS

Your BANKAMERICARD welcome here

Good Man is Not ard to Find

Mobilgas
SOCONY-VACUUM

Navin

EZ-SERVE

Steve Martin in The Jerk, 1979

Navin

WHEN I WAS A KID,
BATHING SUITS
WERE NOT SEXY. THEY WERE
CALLED TRUNKS; THEY LOOKED
LIKE A SHORTER PAIR OF WALKING
SHORTS. MINE WERE PLAID
MADRAS WITH A LITTLE CLIP
ON THE FRONT AND A
CHANGE POCKET. THEY TOOK
HOURS TO DRY.

Burt Lancaster and Deborah Kerr in From Here to Eternity, *1953*

I'd recommend the basic boxer shape for everybody; the longer surf trunks that have been going in and out of style since the sixties beach movies continue to make statements on and off the sand.

Sean Connery and Margaret Nolan in Goldfinger, 1964

Annette Funicello and Frankie Avalon in Beach Blanket Bingo, 1965

all guys are great in

Jantzen

swim trunks
sunclothes

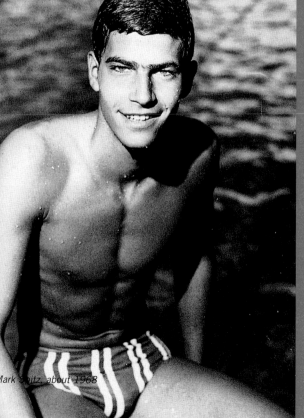

Mark Spitz, about 1968

EIGHT-POUND SUIT

The Jantzen Company, formerly the Portland
Knitting Company, made its first bathing suit
for members of the Portland Rowing Club.
It was a stretchy, ribbed knit wool body suit
that looked like a combination of today's tank
top and bike shorts. It weighed a
whopping eight pounds when wet.
By contrast, the men's racing suit that
originated in Australia in the twenties, now
known generically as the Speedo, weighs less
than eight ounces. The medal sweep of the
1956 Australian Olympic swimming team
brought the Speedo brand worldwide
attention.

SHADES MAKE EVERYONE LOOK COOLER, BUT THE ONLY REASO

Fifties aviator sunglasses. Photograph by Bill Steele

YOU SHOULD WEAR THEM AT NIGHT IS IF YOUR EYES LOOK REALLY TIRED.

Cruise Control

According to Bausch & Lomb, the manufacturer of Ray-Ban sunglasses, its two biggest-selling sunglass styles had their biggest sales years when Tom Cruise wore them in his films. The humble Wayfarer, which had been languishing since its introduction in 1952, became instantly famous in Cruise's RISKY BUSINESS (and went on to define new-wave style on the faces of the Blues Brothers, Madonna, Corey "Sunglasses at Night" Hart, Huey Lewis, and countless others, and to get a name check in Don Henley's song "The Boys of Summer").

The aviator frame (the original Ray-Ban product) was developed for the army air corps, which needed anti-glare goggles for pilots. The aviators were released to the public in 1937, and became Tom Cruise's signature gear in TOP GUN. In JERRY MAGUIRE, Cruise selected a pair of the already hip Arnett, another product by Bausch & Lomb. To launch its newest sunglasses, the Predator 2, Bausch & Lomb outfitted Tommy Lee Jones and Will Smith with shades for their 1997 film MEN IN BLACK.

Rebecca De Mornay and Tom Cruise in Risky Business, *1983 (top); Tom Cruise in* Top Gun, *1986.*

SHADES

In ancient China, judges wore smoky
quartz lenses to hide their facial expressions.
In 1430, when eyeglasses were invented,
some were also darkened. Protective glasses
were developed in the latter half of the
19th century, using mica and amber.
Sunglasses as we now know them were first
created in 1885. In addition to providing
protection from the sun, they have been
widely adopted as fashion statements since
their popularization by Hollywood movie stars
in the thirties and forties.

Dan Aykroyd and John Belushi in The Blues Brothers, *1980*

WHEN IT COMES TO SPECS, HORN RIMS HAVE THE UNIQUE ABILITY TO MAKE A NERD LOOK LIKE A SWINGER AND VICE VERSA.

A Short History of Horn Rims

In the 1700s, the shells of tortoises were carved to hold lenses; today the practice is rare, but the color still survives: the horns of certain animals have been carved into frames known as horn rims. For a pretty penny, you get water-buffalo horn rims—without cruelty, too: water buffalo shed their horns every year. The alternatives are mold-injected plastic or optical-quality frames made from acetate zylonite.

Cary Grant

Woody Allen

Clint Eastwood

Clark Kent

Allen Ginsberg

Jerry Lewis

Buddy Holly

Arthur Ashe

The Specs

How to make them fit your face

You want to make an impression. You want to look strong, handsome, and rich. Like Ari Onassis or Marcello Mastroianni. Or you want to look vulnerable but brainy, nerdy but chic. Like Woody Allen or Elvis Costello.

If you have delicate features, stick with wire rims. Otherwise, remember this: The squarer the frame, the sharper it looks: think Peter Sellers, Arthur Ashe. The rounder, the nerdier: think Jerry Lewis, Harold Lloyd.

If your face is square, try rounder frames. If your face is long, choose a frame that has more depth (the distance from the top to the bottom) than width (the distance from the bridge to the temple). If your face is short, choose a rectangular frame that has more width than depth.

HORN RIMS

Nerd glasses

National Health specs (British)

Buddy Hollies

Clark Kents

Blues Brothers

Engineers' glasses

Sears specials

ATHLETICS

Energy, speed, thrust, the burning desire to win—to me, that's what sports are all about. Athletics bring extreme excitement to American life.

Like most American boys, I had a dream that one day I would be a pro ball player; it didn't really matter which game. I played pitcher, second base, and shortstop in the local Little League, and I started out as safety and ended up becoming quarterback in small-fry football. I collected baseball cards and football cards. I followed our hometown baseball team, the Elmira Pioneers, a farm team for the Orioles. I liked the Orioles, but I liked the Yankees better. I was a fan of Syracuse, Notre Dame, the Cleveland Browns, the Green Bay Packers, and the 49ers, and my heroes were Ernie Davis—the Elmira Express—Jim Brown, Jim Taylor, Mickey Mantle, and Wilt Chamberlain. The rougher sports were very interesting to me; all the grunts and groans, the pushing and shoving. But it came as a rude awakening when I turned 13 and still weighed in at only 90 pounds.

As a teenager, I went on to learn a great deal about sports attire and equipment from my employment in a sporting-goods store, an experience that would eventually inspire much of what I do in all aspects of my collections today. Things weren't so high-tech back then. Tennis rackets were still made of wood, and jerseys were made of wool; college football players wore leather helmets, and a coach could typically be seen running around the field in a long overcoat and wing-tip shoes.

It's interesting how, until recently, sports equipment had been considered so much for its utility alone. That has changed dramatically, especially after urban kids put their stamp of approval on athletic clothes by wearing them off the fields and courts and on the streets. It began with hero worship—the desire to emulate one's favorite athlete or as a pure expression of support for a team—and ended up as one of the most significant fashion statements of the nineties.

Meanwhile, the traditions of the English gentleman's sports, polo, cricket, and hunting, the country life pursuits, continue to exert their big attraction. Polo matches are thrilling to watch—the clumping noise and awesome power of the horses running across the field. There's a certain aura around the sport; the spectators are so interesting in the way they dress, putting on their own exclusive fashion show. The world of antique sports equipment and art is inspiring as well—the old wool baseball jerseys which have evolved into casual American sportswear, and the cricket uniforms of the past, which gave us today's tennis sweater. Mixing these with elements of the high-tech uniforms of today brings me something totally different.

When I was a kid, there were no Rollerblades or snowboards, and windsurfing was unheard of. I learned to ski with leather boots and wooden skis on the icy slopes of a local resort in upstate New York. Today's modern-miracle materials let you achieve peak performance no matter what level you're at: boots that hold your feet in the best position for downhill, underwear that wicks away perspiration, Ultrex jackets that are windproof but breathable. In my sports clothing, I first aim for authentic details and then I make sure it's functional. After that, I care about the style. Whether it's a logoed sailing jacket or a hockey or a rugby jersey, authenticity is what matters most to people. As opposed to regular clothes, this look says you're a player on the team, even if you aren't.

AS KIDS, WE THOUGHT IT WAS NEAT TO SNEAK OUT OF BOWLING ALLEYS WITH A PAIR OF BOWLING SHOES TO WEAR WITH OUR JEANS. BUT THE EMBROIDERED SHIRTS ARE THE THING THAT REALLY SIGNIFY THAT IT'S A GOOD-TIME SPORT.

COLLARS
Are often in contrasting colors to the body of the shirt. On some shirts, the figure of a bowler is embroidered on the collar.

SLEEVE HEMS
Usually come in contrasting colors.

EMBROIDERED NAME
Always goes above the pocket; team logo goes on back.

CLASSIC CUT
Is boxy, to allow for a full swing. Some shirt bodies have contrasting front panels; others have a different colored yoke across the front and back shoulders.

BUTTONS
Often match the color of the collar. On some old shirts, buttons are shaped like bowling pins.

CUSTOMIZE YOUR BOWLING SHIRT

You can buy bowling shirts from most pro shops and bowling-supply stores, as well as from some sporting-goods outlets. Both the American Bowling Congress and the Professional Bowling Association have their own lines, most of which can be custom screen-printed or embroidered with your name and logo.

You can also have your pro shop order basic shirts from

Hilton Active Apparel (847-675-1010). For classics, try placing an order with King Louie (816-765-5212), who feature three cotton-poly shirt styles: The Kramer (a basic body with contrasting collars and buttons in five color combos and an embroidered bowler on the collar); The Turbo (blue, red, or black with matching epaulets and collar on a white front and back yoke); and The Blackburn (with a square shirttail and

Memory Lanes

The most striking bowling sites in America

BILTMORE HOUSE
Asheville, North Carolina. Built in 1895 in the basement rec room of railroad millionaire Cornelius Vanderbilt's house. For strolling, not rolling.

HOLLER HOUSE
Milwaukee, Wisconsin. Two lanes, human pinsetters, and a chalkboard for scoring. Built in 1910.

PIONEER BOWL
Yucca Valley, California. Built in 1947 in Pioneertown, a famous setting for Hollywood westerns. Vintage equipment.

FIESTA BOWL
Highway 27, Lady Lake, Florida. This alley, built in 1990, is styled to look like the Spanish-Mexican mission in San Antonio.

COUNTRY MART LANES
Leon, West Virginia. Four lanes in a mini-mart/hardware store.

SHOWBOAT HOTEL AND CASINO
Las Vegas, Nevada. Want to roll a few frames Christmas Day? No problem here. 106 lanes. Never closed.

NATIONAL BOWLING HALL OF FAME AND MUSEUM
St. Louis, Missouri. Houses a collection of over 750 bowling shirts.

ROBERT LEE KNIGHT'S BOWLING HALL OF FAME
Colorado Springs, Colorado. One of the biggest private collections of memorabilia. Free tours.

ROSSI LANES
Washington Avenue, Elmira, New York. Where I learned how to bowl.

DIXIE LANES
Caton Avenue, Elmira, New York. Where my dad bowled on Schreibman Jewelers' teams.

contrasting front panels; derived from an English soccer team's uniform).

To order your own shirt direct, call Classic Products (219-484-2695), which does hand embroidery and silkscreen printing of names and logos (as long as they're not trademarked) on a variety of shirt styles (no minimums, but two weeks' processing time).

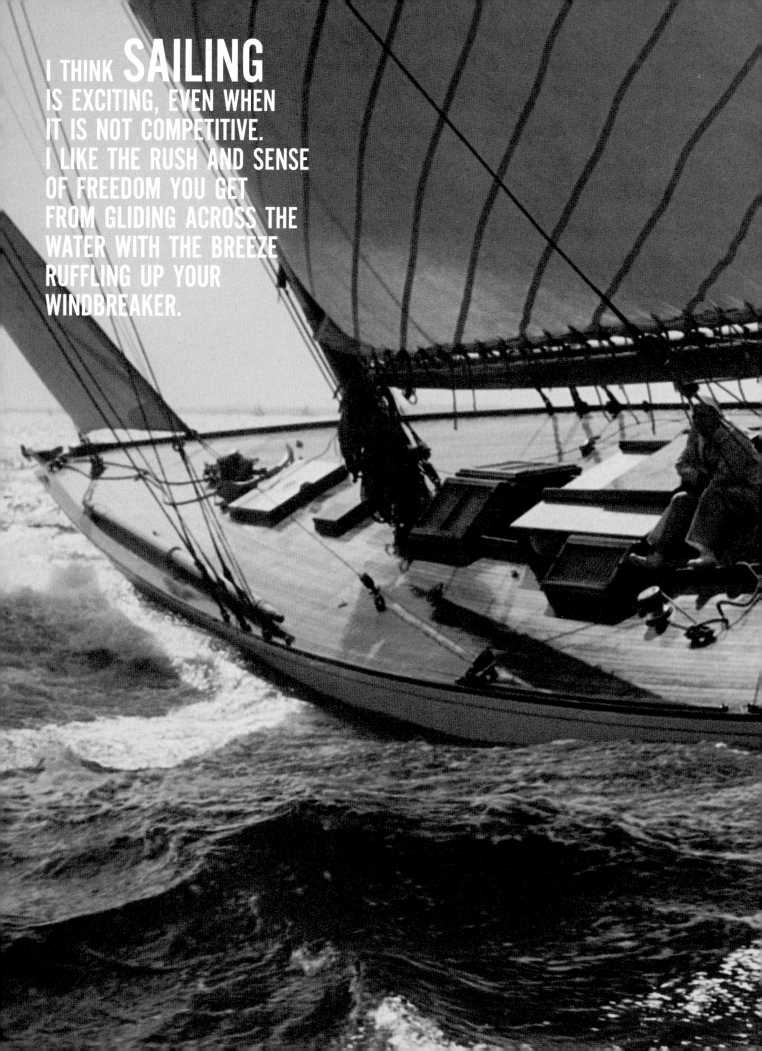

I THINK **SAILING** IS EXCITING, EVEN WHEN IT IS NOT COMPETITIVE. I LIKE THE RUSH AND SENSE OF FREEDOM YOU GET FROM GLIDING ACROSS THE WATER WITH THE BREEZE RUFFLING UP YOUR WINDBREAKER.

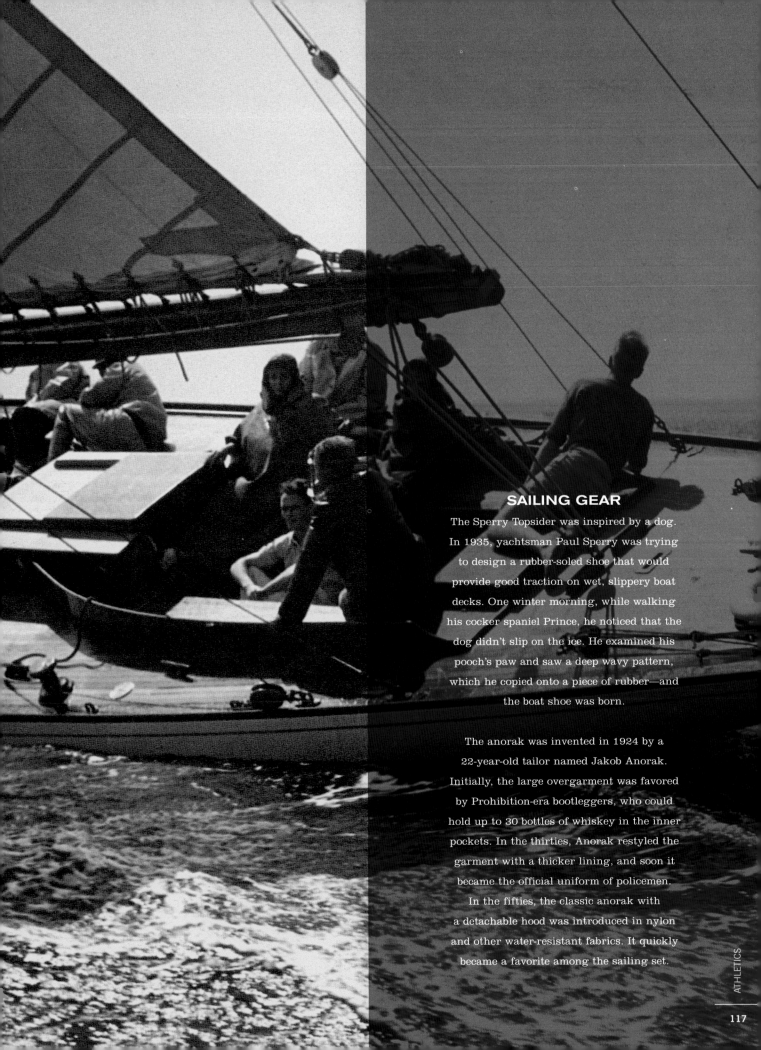

SAILING GEAR

The Sperry Topsider was inspired by a dog.
In 1935, yachtsman Paul Sperry was trying
to design a rubber-soled shoe that would
provide good traction on wet, slippery boat
decks. One winter morning, while walking
his cocker spaniel Prince, he noticed that the
dog didn't slip on the ice. He examined his
pooch's paw and saw a deep wavy pattern,
which he copied onto a piece of rubber—and
the boat shoe was born.

The anorak was invented in 1924 by a
22-year-old tailor named Jakob Anorak.
Initially, the large overgarment was favored
by Prohibition-era bootleggers, who could
hold up to 30 bottles of whiskey in the inner
pockets. In the thirties, Anorak restyled the
garment with a thicker lining, and soon it
became the official uniform of policemen.
In the fifties, the classic anorak with
a detachable hood was introduced in nylon
and other water-resistant fabrics. It quickly
became a favorite among the sailing set.

President John F. Kennedy

THE SAILING WARDROBE

Oilskins (water-resistant, foul-weather gear, also known as oilies)   Hooded anorak (pullover or zip-front styles)   Windproof and waterproof, breathable jacket with Velcro closures   Nylon overalls or pull-on pants   Polar-fleece sweaters or vests   Deck shoes   Helly Hanson jacket

VELCRO

Velcro was invented in 1948 by a Swiss mountaineer named George de Mestral, who returned from an alpine walk covered in cockleburs. While picking them off his socks and pants, he discovered that they were covered with thousands of tiny hooks that clung to the fibers of his clothing. He then designed a fastening system based on his discovery and took its name from the French "velour crochet," which means "velvet hook."

The Nautical Flag Lexicon
Graphics that really say something

**Keep Well Clear
at Low Speed**

**I Am Carrying
Dangerous Goods**

Yes (Affirmative)

**I Am Maneuvering
With Difficulty**

**I Am Directing My
Course to Starboard**

**I Am Disabled;
Communicate With Me**

I Require a Pilot

**I Have a Pilot
On Board**

**I Am Directing My
Course to Port**

**I Am on Fire;
Keep Clear of Me**

**I Have Something
to Communicate**

**You Should Stop
Your Vessel**

**My Vessel Is
Stopped**

No (Negative)

Man Overboard

**All Persons to
Report on Board**

**I Request Free
Pratique**

No Meaning

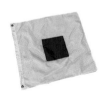

**My Engines Are Going
Full Speed Astern**

**You Are Running
Into Danger**

**I Require
Assistance**

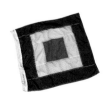

**I Require Medical
Assistance**

**Stop Carrying Out
Your Intentions**

I Require a Tug

WHEN I WAS GROWING UP,
I LIVED FOR SATURDAY-AFTERNOON COLLEGE
FOOTBALL
GAMES. IT WAS BEST WHEN THE WEATHER
WAS BRISK AND WE WERE ALL BUNDLED UP
IN STADIUM COATS OR DUFFLES.

High school football, Seattle, Washington. Photograph by Burt Glinn, 1955

Post-game embrace. Photograph by Burt Glinn, 1955

Michigan **Wolverines** North Carolina (Chapel Hill) **Tar Heels** Akron **Zips** Montana **Grizzlies** Kentucky **Wildcats** Florida **Gators** Pennsylvania State **Nittany Lions** Nebraska **Cornhuskers** Tennessee State **Tigers** University of Tennessee **Volunteers** Minnesota **Golden Gophers** Hawaii **Rainbow Warriors** University of Wisconsin **Badgers** Auburn **Tigers** University of Arkansas **Razorbacks** Georgia **Bulldogs** Purdue **Boilermakers** Virginia Tech **Gobblers** Duke **Blue Devils** Kansas State **Wildcats** University of Connecticut **Huskies** North Texas **Mean Green** Virginia **Cavaliers** Arizona **Wildcats** Arizona State **Sun Devils** Texas Christian **Horned Frogs** Cincinnati **Bearcats** South Carolina **Fighting Gamecocks** Clemson **Tigers** Maryland **Terrapins** Kent State **Golden Flashes** Georgia Tech **Yellow Jackets** Mississippi State **Bulldogs** North Carolina State **Wolfpack** New Mexico **Lobos** Oklahoma State **Cowboys** Mississippi **Ole Miss Rebels** Pittsburgh **Panthers** Boston College **Eagles**

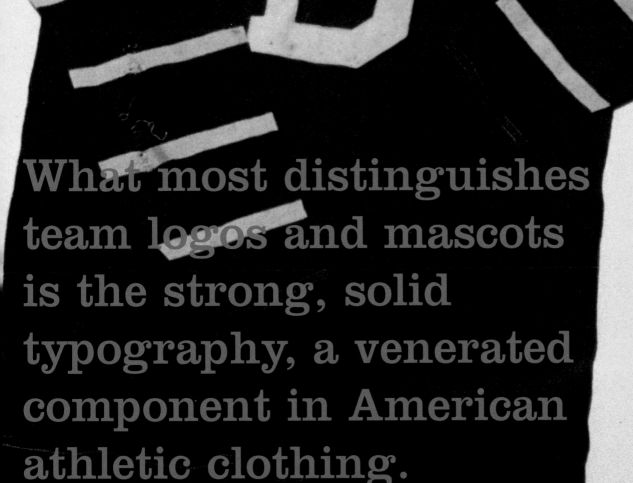

What most distinguishes team logos and mascots is the strong, solid typography, a venerated component in American athletic clothing.

Cleveland Brown Jim Brown. Photograph by Robert Riger, 1958 (courtesy of James Danziger Gallery)

Green Bay Packer Forrest Gregg. Photograph by Robert Riger, 1960 (courtesy of James Danziger Gallery)

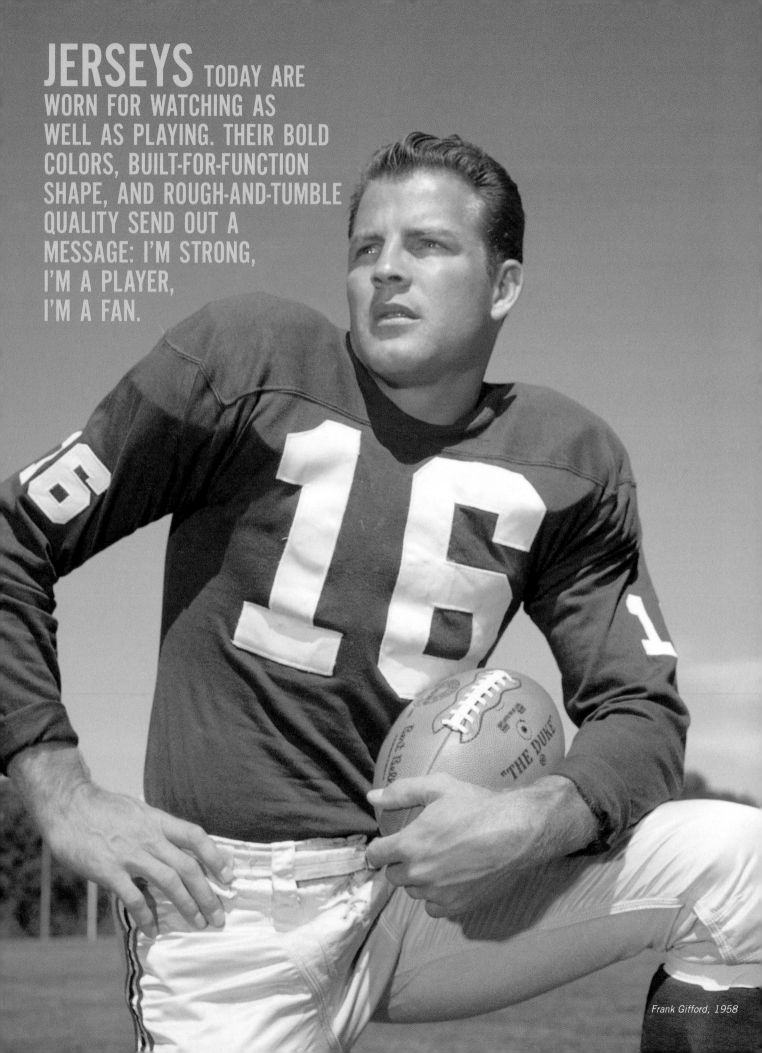

JERSEYS TODAY ARE WORN FOR WATCHING AS WELL AS PLAYING. THEIR BOLD COLORS, BUILT-FOR-FUNCTION SHAPE, AND ROUGH-AND-TUMBLE QUALITY SEND OUT A MESSAGE: I'M STRONG, I'M A PLAYER, I'M A FAN.

Frank Gifford, 1958

Mick Jagger, 1981

The Jerseys:
American Style

HOCKEY

Oversized (to fit over padding)
V-neck
Contrast-colored yokes
Team number on the back
Embroidered team name and logo
on the front
Quick-drying nylon
Square hem

FOOTBALL

Perforated cotton or nylon
High V-neck (formerly crew necks)
Stripes on the sleeve
Player number on the back
Team name on the front
Square hem

BASKETBALL

Sleeveless (to allow maximum
shoulder movement)
Double rows of piping
Team name on the front
Player name and number
on the back
Baggy shorts (thanks to
Michael Jordan)
Side-vented hem

BASEBALL

Pajama-type front
Ribbing or piping
Collarless
Pin stripes
Baseball cap
Stockings
Short, wide sleeves
Rounded shirttails

Sports fashion was blessed by kids yearning to look like their favorite athlete. Now it's part of the vocabulary of casual style and an element of the rock and roll and hip-hop wardrobe for stars and fans alike.

L. L. Cool J

MICKEY SHIRT

In 1991 a privately owned flannel jersey that was originally worn by Mickey Mantle was put up for auction at $50,000; it sold for $71,500.

New York Yankee Mickey Mantle, 1955

GOLFERS ARE AS CONCERNED WITH WHAT THEY WEAR AS WITH THEIR GAME. IF THEY CAN'T PLAY, AT LEAST THEY MUST LOOK GOOD.

GOLF SHIRTS

ARE VERY CLASSIC, BUT THEY ALSO DECLARE, "LOOK AT ME, I'M A LITTLE BIT MORE COLORFUL THAN THE OTHER GOLFERS." A GOLF COURSE IS THE ONLY PLACE WHERE A PINK SWEATER WITH PLAID PANTS DOES NOT GET A SECOND LOOK.

SLEEVE
Hemmed, not banded, to allow maximum freedom while swinging.

Fifties golf shirt with specialized tee pocket. Photograph by Bill Steele

BUTTON LOOP
Rarely used, it
provides a clean line
between the collar
and placket.

LOOPS
Hold golf tees in place.

POCKET
Holds scorecards;
button keeps them from
falling out when
bending over.

SIDE VENT
Allows for twisting
motion when swinging
woods and irons.

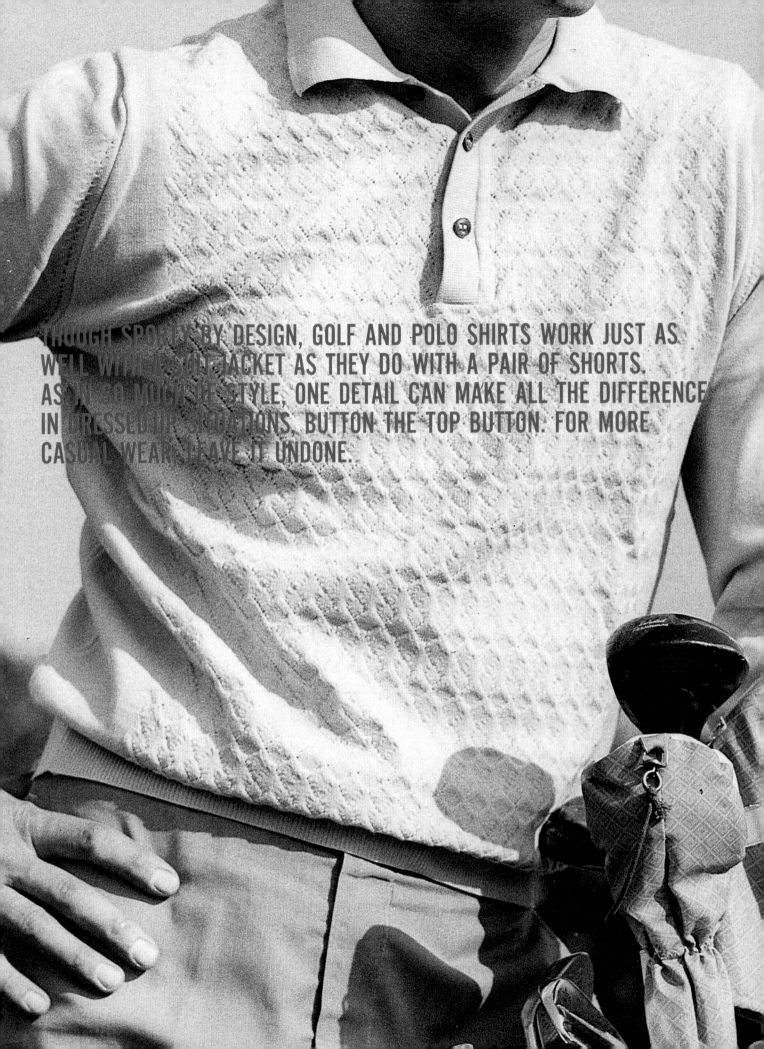

THOUGH SPORTY BY DESIGN, GOLF AND POLO SHIRTS WORK JUST AS WELL WITH A SUIT JACKET AS THEY DO WITH A PAIR OF SHORTS. AS IN SO MUCH OF STYLE, ONE DETAIL CAN MAKE ALL THE DIFFERENCE IN DRESSED UP SITUATIONS, BUTTON THE TOP BUTTON. FOR MORE CASUAL WEAR, LEAVE IT UNDONE.

LOGO HALL OF FAME

Choose your badges of honor

Lacoste—Crocodile

Munsingwear—Penguin

Brooks Brothers—Golden fleece

Tommy Hilfiger—Crest

Ralph Lauren—Polo player

Ashworth—Golfer

Greg Norman—Shark

Nautica—Sailboat

Sahara—Camel

Slazenger—Panther

Cobra—Snake

Pine Valley Golf Club—Shield

Augusta National—U.S. map

Merion Golf Club—Wicker basket

Quaker Ridge—Quaker

Kapalua Resort—Butterfly

Ko-Olina Resort—Ladybug

THE GOOD-SPORT SHIRT

The original shirt that polo players wore was a lightweight, long-sleeve woolen jersey. The difference between today's short-sleeve polo shirt (derived from tennis shirts of the early 1900s) and a golf shirt is simple. The polo has a banded sleeve hem, which hugs the arm, while the golf shirt has a loose sleeve, a slightly fuller cut, and a pocket.

WHEN I WAS GROWING UP, TENNIS CLOTHES COULD BE SUMMED UP IN TWO WORDS: WHITE AND TIGHT.

At Your Service

In the beginning, tennis players wore jerseys with knickers. During the first U.S. nationals in 1881, men wore white flannel pants. Nearer the end of the century, they adopted single-breasted jackets and white or blue striped flannel trousers, as well as rubber-soled canvas shoes. In 1926, René Lacoste, known as "le Crocodile," scandalized the tennis world by wearing a short-sleeved knit tennis shirt (looking very much like today's polos) at the 1926 Davis Cup championship. It had a long tail in the back, which ensured that the shirt would stay tucked in when serving or going for a lob. The first person to wear tennis shorts during competition was H. W. "Bunny" Austin in 1932 at Forest Hills. After World War II, tennis clothes consisted of white cotton shorts and tennis shirts and sweaters. Today, tennis attire has stepped away from traditional whites to splashy colors on high-tech fabrics, while classic whites remain a staple of the preppy wardrobe.

René Lacoste

TENNIS DRESS

The tennis sweater originally had stripes in order to distinguish between members of different tennis clubs or university teams. (The tennis sweater was derived from cricket, another sport traditionally played in white clothing and with team or school colors on the neck and cuffs.) In the twenties, Broadway plays frequently featured a young leading man who would burst onto stage wearing a striped V-neck sweater, saying "Tennis, anyone?" but it was the dandy Prince of Wales, later Edward VIII, who popularized tennis sweaters off the courts.

Tennis star Bill Tilden in the forties

DURING GRAND PRIX SEASON, I WOULD GO TO WATKINS GLEN TO WATCH THE

RACING.

ALL THE DRIVERS LOOKED HEROIC IN THEIR UNIFORMS—COVERED IN PATCHES AND WITH THEIR CARS EMBLAZONED WITH LOGOS. EVEN THE PIT CREW LOOKED SHARP. ONCE, AFTER A RACE, I WENT INTO THE PIT AND BOUGHT A CREW MEMBER'S UNIFORM RIGHT OFF HIS BACK. I PUT IT ON IMMEDIATELY. IT WAS STILL DAMP WITH MOTOR OIL AND HIS PERSPIRATION— I WOULDN'T HAVE EVEN CONSIDERED WASHING IT . . . IT WAS THE BEST $20 I EVER SPENT.

Leather motocross pants. Photograph by Bill Steele

The bold colors, shapes, and graphics of racing gear have left the track and become part of our street style. The wearer's message is the most powerful brew of function, fashion, and speed.

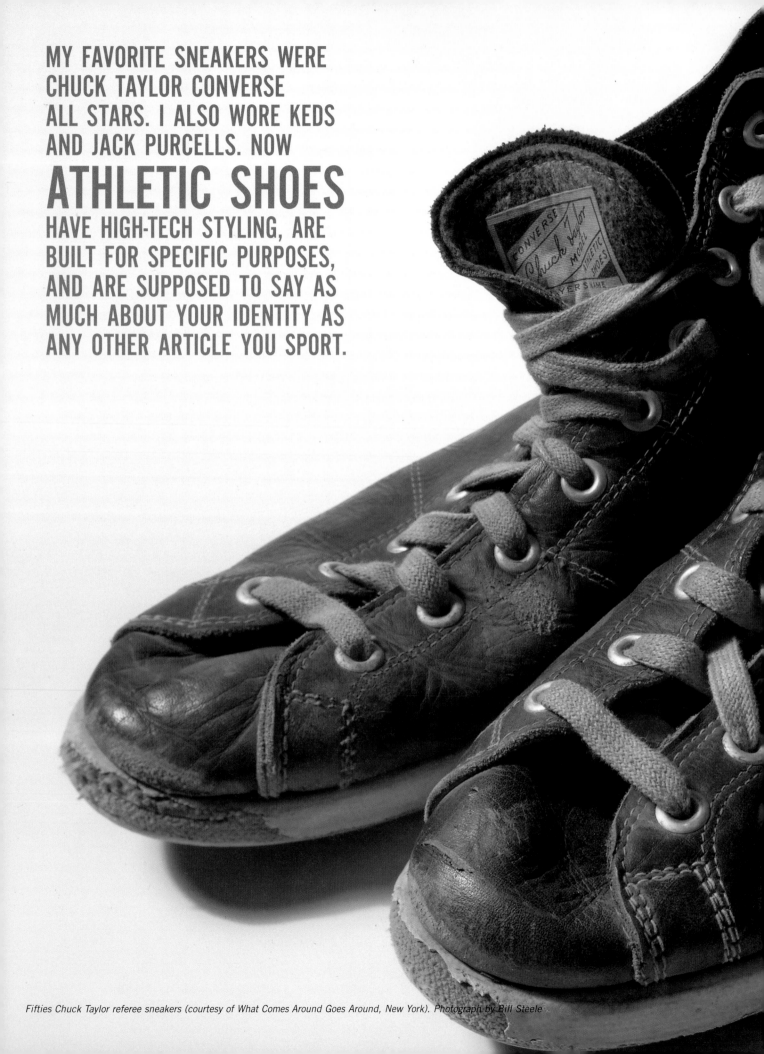

MY FAVORITE SNEAKERS WERE CHUCK TAYLOR CONVERSE ALL STARS. I ALSO WORE KEDS AND JACK PURCELLS. NOW **ATHLETIC SHOES** HAVE HIGH-TECH STYLING, ARE BUILT FOR SPECIFIC PURPOSES, AND ARE SUPPOSED TO SAY AS MUCH ABOUT YOUR IDENTITY AS ANY OTHER ARTICLE YOU SPORT.

Fifties Chuck Taylor referee sneakers (courtesy of What Comes Around Goes Around, New York). Photograph by Bill Steele

MAGIC FEET

In the collection of the Basketball Hall of Fame, Springfield, Massachusetts

Forties Converse All Stars

Wilt Chamberlain's size 15 Converse (worn 1971–72)

Magic Johnson's size 15 Converse (worn 1985–86)

Larry Bird's size 14 Converse (worn 1985–86)

Isiah Thomas's size 12 1/2 Asics (worn 1993–94)

Michael Jordan's size 13 Nikes (worn 1995–96)

Scottie Pippen's size 16 Nikes (worn 1995–96)

Charles Barkley's size 16 Nikes (worn 1995–96)

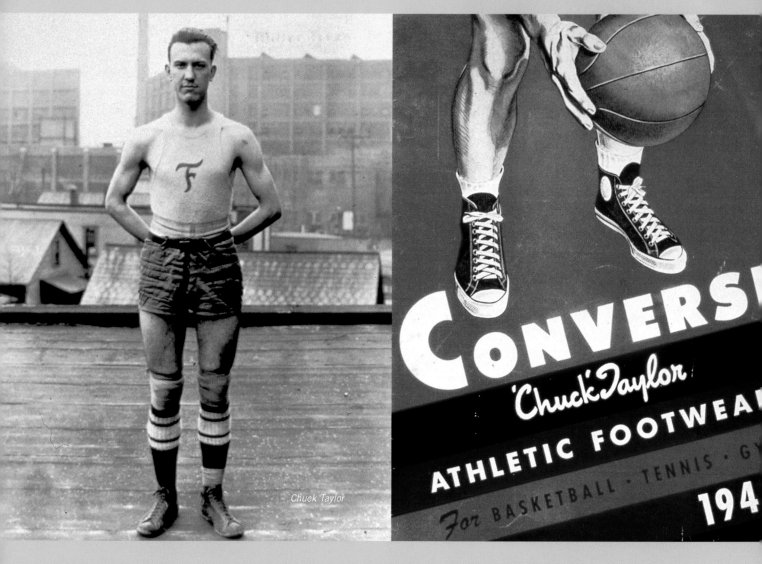

Chuck Taylor

CONVERSE
'Chuck' Taylor
ATHLETIC FOOTWEAR
For BASKETBALL · TENNIS · GY
194

<u>ALL-TIME BEST</u> Adidas Finalist Adidas Formula 1 Adidas Nite Jogger Adidas Stan Smith Adidas Super Star
Converse All Star Converse Chris Evert Etonic Street Fighter Fila Grant Hills New Balance 320 Nike Air Jordans Nike
Elite Nike Huarache Nike LD-100 Nike Pippens Pro-Keds Royal Puma Easy Rider Reebok Aerobic Reebok DMX

SNEAKERS 101

How to shop for athletic shoes

Take your old ones in with you and tell the salesman what you like and don't like about them. Wear the socks you'll actually be wearing with them. Describe to the salesman the activities you'll be pursuing in the shoes. Make sure that the shoe feels good from the moment you put it on. Check that there is adequate room in the toe box, that the shoe does not pinch your arch, and that your ankle feels well supported. Stand up, walk around, jump around. Shop late; feet swell up during the day.

How to care for athletic shoes

While most people routinely throw canvas sneakers into the washing machine, this is not recommended. It is far better to stuff them with paper or cloth so they maintain their shape, handwash them with a mild detergent (adding bleach for whites) and a soft brush, rinse, and restuff the shoes and allow them to air-dry. You can also buy commercial shoe shampoos, available from such manufacturers as Kiwi. For leather shoes, there are a multitude of cleaners, conditioners, and polishes, but since many of today's sports shoes are made of multiple fabrics and colors, the best solution is to have them professionally cleaned.

Michael Jordan, 1997

CATCHERS ALWAYS WORE THEIR
BASEBALL CAPS
BACKWARDS, BUT I DON'T THINK
THAT'S WHY KIDS STARTED
DOING IT. I THINK IT WAS BOTH
PRACTICAL AND STYLISH.
IF THEY WERE PLAYING
BASKETBALL, IT HELPED
THEM SEE THE HOOP;
IF THEY WERE OUT WITH
GIRLS, IT MADE THEIR
FACES EASIER TO SEE,
BUT I THINK MAINLY IT'S
BECAUSE THEY WANTED TO
LOOK IRREVERENT, LIKE
THEY DIDN'T PLAY BY
THE RULES.

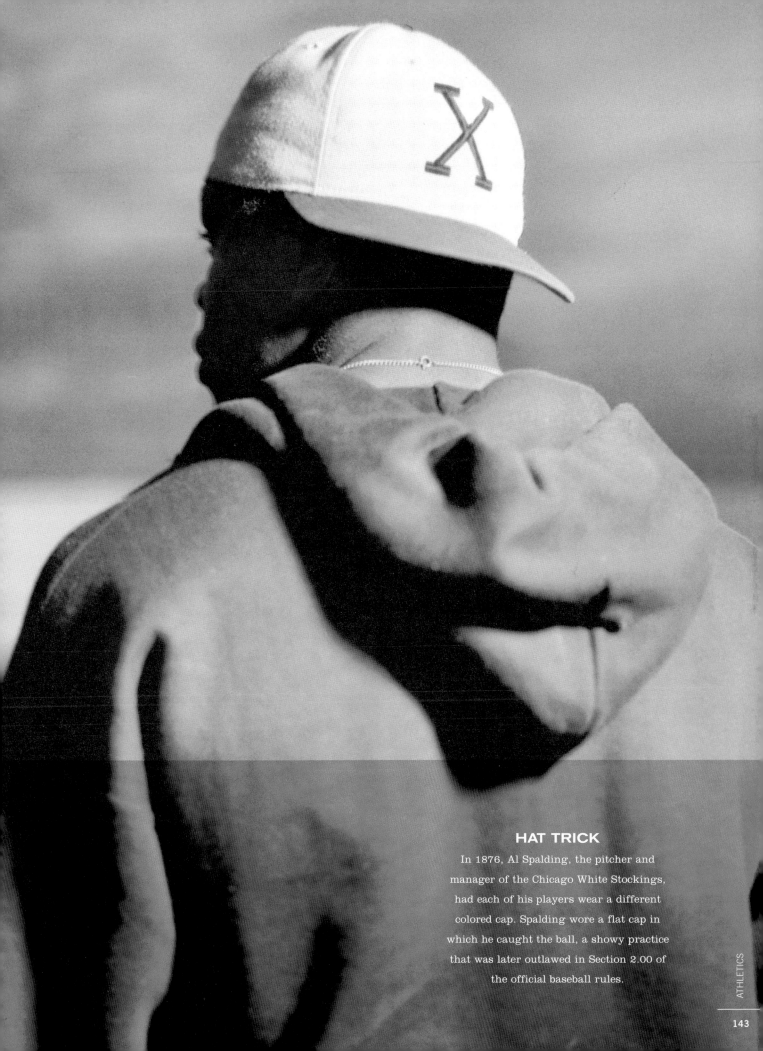

HAT TRICK

In 1876, Al Spalding, the pitcher and manager of the Chicago White Stockings, had each of his players wear a different colored cap. Spalding wore a flat cap in which he caught the ball, a showy practice that was later outlawed in Section 2.00 of the official baseball rules.

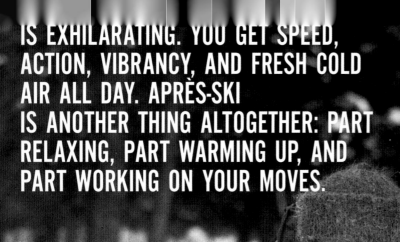

IS EXHILARATING. YOU GET SPEED, ACTION, VIBRANCY, AND FRESH COLD AIR ALL DAY. APRÈS-SKI IS ANOTHER THING ALTOGETHER: PART RELAXING, PART WARMING UP, AND PART WORKING ON YOUR MOVES.

SKIWEAR STAPLES

Clothes we were inclined to wear

Stocking caps

Puffy parkas

Dmitri sweaters
 (as worn by Spyder Sabitch)

Reindeer sweaters

Snowflake-pattern sweaters

Spider-brand ski sweaters
 (with padding on the
 shoulders and arms)

Turtlenecks

Racing-stripe sweaters

Snowboarding shorts

Long johns

Wool ski pants

Topping
It Off

In the beginning, ski caps served one purpose: to keep your head and ears warm. Ever since skiing became a popular middle-class sport in the U.S., the ski cap has shifted sizes and shapes from long stocking (now made in polar fleece) to pom-pomed wool (like the one Michael Nesmith wore in every episode of The Monkees), to the standard blunt-top watch cap, which began as a nighttime warmer-upper for sea-men and became a favorite among rappers and slackers alike.

Above: Michael Nesmith of the Monkees

Peter Fonda in Easy Rider, *1969*

SOUND+VISION

I see everything through the pop-culture lens.

It all started innocently enough, with Disney movies, family TV shows like Dennis the Menace and My Three Sons. I liked watching westerns and sports as well as suspense shows like The Twilight Zone—Rod Serling always looked so perfectly put together. I was very impressed with Sean Connery in the early James Bond films, and the clothes in THE SOUND OF MUSIC have been an inspiration for my winter collections. But when the Beatles arrived, they changed my life. I wanted to grow my hair long and to be in a band. I saw A HARD DAY'S NIGHT and was forever captivated.

English rock has influenced me totally. It's something I grew up with—I think I was the first kid to discover it in my high school—and it has been with me ever since. By the mid-sixties, I was getting into a real mod headset; all the rock and roll bands were my influence and I wanted to look like them. The more showy they were, the more interesting they were to me. I wasn't into looking at bands in jeans and T-shirts; even if I liked their music, there was a lack of appeal. I liked a band with an eclectic look, like the Stones: Mick had his unique sexiness; Brian Jones was wearing smocks and frocks; Charlie Watts was always crisply tailored. Even the Beatles, though they dressed

alike, had their signature items: John Lennon's Greek fisherman's cap, Ringo's rings. I went for the dandy look of the Kinks. And I worshiped the Who, Blind Faith, and Traffic; they were much more irreverent than the American groups.

It took a while, but by the late sixties American rock groups started showing signs of style. Jefferson Airplane and the Doors looked and sounded fantastic. Musicians were beginning to embrace fashion in a way they never had before. Hendrix was an innovator. Still, the British bands were continually breaking new ground. I found Deep Purple, the Small Faces, Spooky Tooth, and Jethro Tull inspired me. Rod Stewart took things to a higher level. The Who were operatic, and Led Zeppelin, as they sang, paved a stairway to heaven. But then Bowie and T-Rex came along and the whole look changed. Androgyny was in; glitter rocked. By that time I had moved to New York and was going to shops like Jumpin' Jack Flash, Granny Takes a Trip, and Limbo, which were the places to go for real serious rock and roll clothes. I was wearing snakeskin high-heeled platforms, velvet bell bottoms that were low-cut, very tight at the hips, and flared out at the bottom. I wore midriff tops so you could see my stomach. One of my tops had a star on it; I wore another that was ribbed, together with a jacket that had round lapels, just like Rod Stewart used to wear.

A few years later, when punk started happening in the underground, I got a spiky haircut and got into the Ramones, the Police, the Cars, and the whole new-wave scene. But I didn't love that as much as I loved the Studio 54 disco era. And then I started hearing rap: music and poetry, filled with pride and anger and adventure. Like the Motown artists, like Jimi Hendrix, like the outrageous funk bands of the seventies. The sense of style that rappers exhibited was terrific. It was, and is, a combination of designer goods and athletic clothes that were functional and accessible, and that transformed street kids into sporty superheroes—Run DMC and their Adidas, the Beastie Boys wearing Volkswagen hood ornaments as medallions, and then all the rappers wearing designer and sports logos, from Louis Vuitton to Nike.

Today, American music and arts are one big glorious mix of iconography. Everybody borrows from one another, and everybody wants to get in on the act. It's easy to see why rappers and kids like to dress like sports heroes, and why sports stars like to make movies and records and design their own clothes. Pop culture feeds on change. These are some of the moments I've been through, the styles that now seem classic and that continue to inform me.

WHEN **ROCK AND ROLL** BEGAN, LEGENDS LIKE JOHN LEE HOOKER, CHUCK BERRY, BO DIDDLEY, AND B. B. KING DRESSED TO KILL. THE R&B STARS WANTED SHINE, SEQUINS, GLAM; THEY WANTED POINTY-TOED SHOES. JUST PICTURE LITTLE RICHARD IN THE SEQUINED SUITS; THAT WAS FASHION WAY BEFORE GLAM CAME ON THE SCENE.

Chuck Berry

Bo Diddley

B. B. King

John Lee Hooker

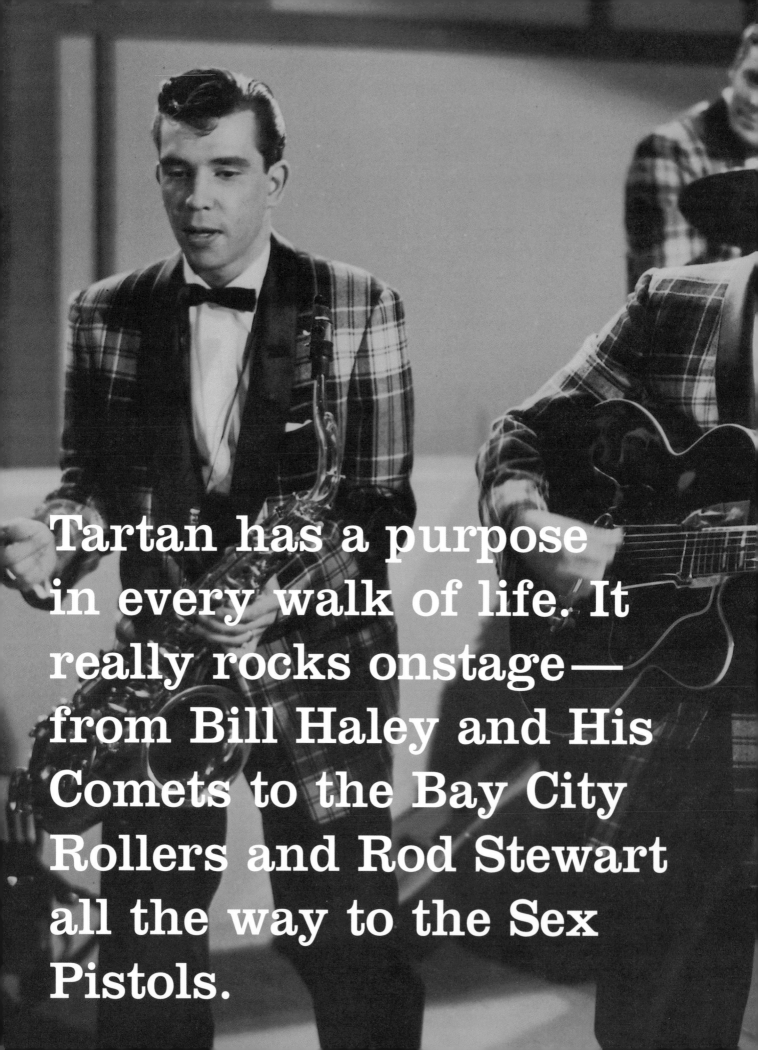

Tartan has a purpose in every walk of life. It really rocks onstage—from Bill Haley and His Comets to the Bay City Rollers and Rod Stewart all the way to the Sex Pistols.

Bill Haley and His Comets

Chubby Checker

James Brown

DANCING, HOWEVER, JAMES BROWN HAD BOTH THE LOOKS AND THE MOVES.

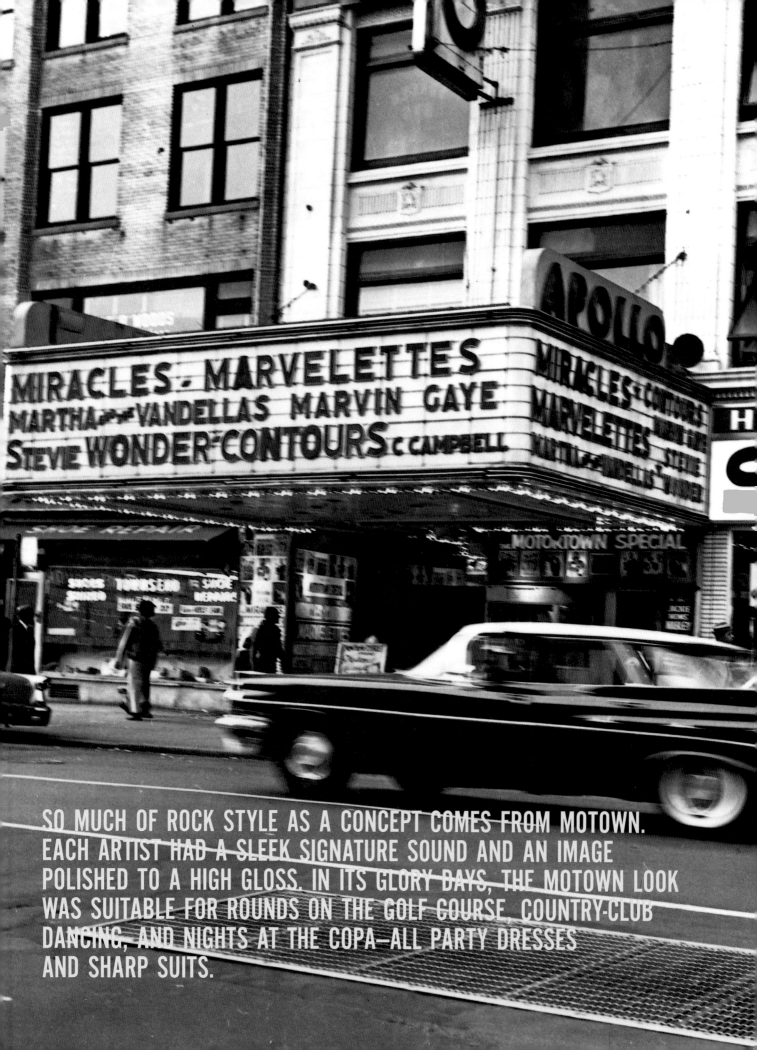

SO MUCH OF ROCK STYLE AS A CONCEPT COMES FROM MOTOWN.
EACH ARTIST HAD A SLEEK SIGNATURE SOUND AND AN IMAGE
POLISHED TO A HIGH GLOSS. IN ITS GLORY DAYS, THE MOTOWN LOOK
WAS SUITABLE FOR ROUNDS ON THE GOLF COURSE, COUNTRY-CLUB
DANCING, AND NIGHTS AT THE COPA—ALL PARTY DRESSES
AND SHARP SUITS.

The Temptations

Stevie Wonder

Smokey Robinson and the Miracles

THE MOTOWN SOUND

They looked as good as they sang

The Supremes

Smokey Robinson and the Miracles

The Temptations

Stevie Wonder

The Four Tops

Marvin Gaye

Martha and the Vandellas

Mary Wells

THE RAT PACK
GAVE ELEGANCE
A NEW DEFINITION:
SHINY SHARKSKIN
SUITS,
SKINNY LAPELS,
THIN TIES, SLIM
PANTS, AND THE
KIND OF HATS MEN
WOULD WEAR TO
THE RACETRACK.

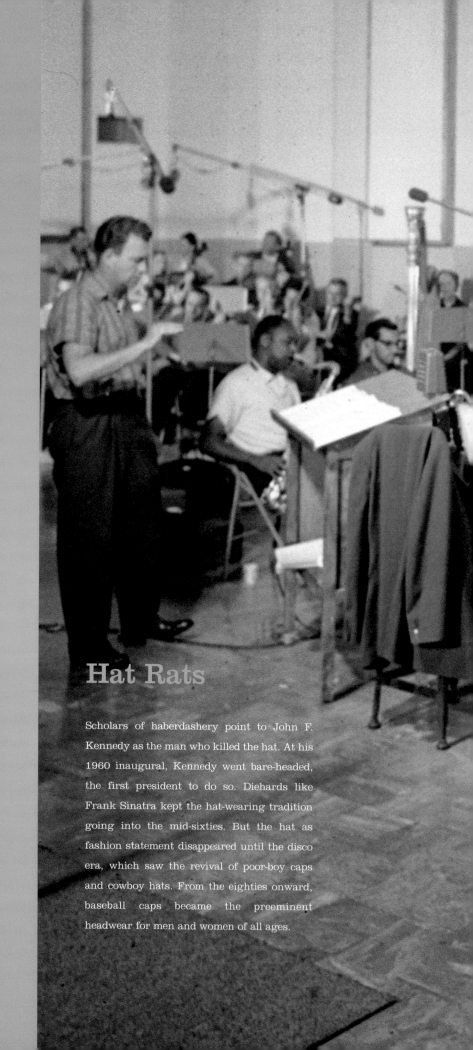

Hat Rats

Scholars of haberdashery point to John F. Kennedy as the man who killed the hat. At his 1960 inaugural, Kennedy went bare-headed, the first president to do so. Diehards like Frank Sinatra kept the hat-wearing tradition going into the mid-sixties. But the hat as fashion statement disappeared until the disco era, which saw the revival of poor-boy caps and cowboy hats. From the eighties onward, baseball caps became the preeminent headwear for men and women of all ages.

Sammy Davis, Jr.

SHARP DRESSERS

You could do worse than to
look like them

Cast of The Man From Uncle

Cast of Mission Impossible

Cast of RESERVOIR DOGS

Sammy Davis, Jr.

Sean Connery

Dean Martin

Frank Sinatra

Peter Lawford

Fred Astaire

Rod Serling

Jerry Lewis

Tom Jones

Rod Serling

Mission Impossible

Sean Connery in Thunderball, 1965

Reservoir Dogs, 1992

THE BEATLES AND THE ROLLING STONES WERE AT THE FOREFRONT OF THE MOD REVOLUTION. BOTH GROUPS REDEFINED WHAT MEN COULD WEAR AND CREATED A KALEIDOSCOPIC ROCK STYLE THROUGH THEIR ROCK STARDOM.

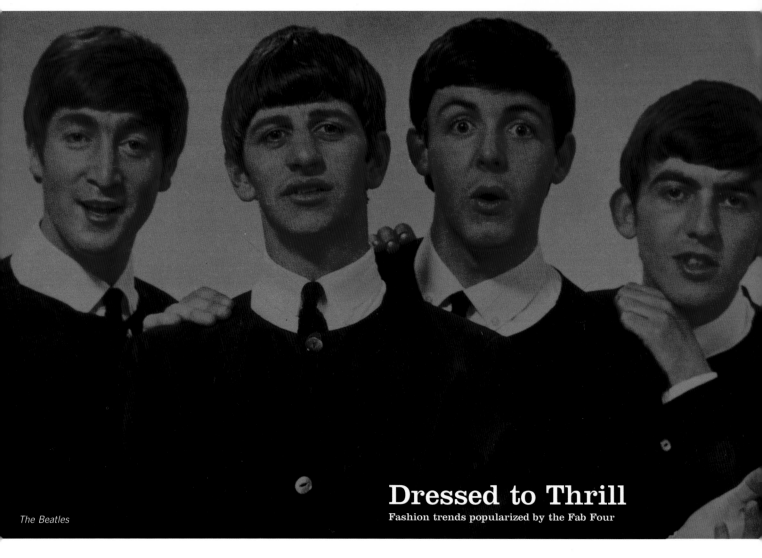

The Beatles

Dressed to Thrill
Fashion trends popularized by the Fab Four

Mop-top haircuts (a long variation of the Caesar)

Big smiles

Collarless jackets

Jackets without lapels

Beatle boots (also known as Chelsea boots)

Greek fisherman's caps (John Lennon)

Flashy rings (Ringo Starr)

Suede jackets (Rubber Soul era)

Band uniforms and mustaches (Sgt. Pepper's)

Wire-rim glasses (John and Yoko Ono)

Beards (Let It Be)

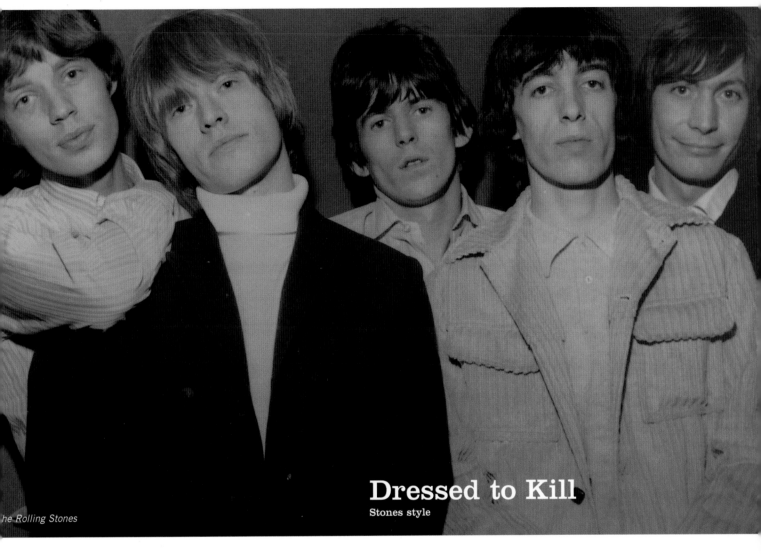

The Rolling Stones

Dressed to Kill

Stones style

Shaggy hair and Prince Valiant cuts

Big lips

Tight jeans

Turtlenecks and tab-collar shirts

Velvet jackets

Edwardian shirts

Pin-stripe suits and polka dots (Brian Jones)

Skull rings (Keith Richards)

Army uniforms

Capezios

Long scarves

Funky corduroys

Paisleys and foulards

Jumpsuits

Athletic wear

They seek him here, they seek him there,
His clothes are loud, but never square.
It will make or break him so he's got to buy the best,
'Cos he's a dedicated follower of fashion. . . .
And when he does his little rounds
'Round the boutiques of London Town,
Eagerly pursuing all the latest fads and trends,
'Cause he's a dedicated follower of fashion.

—The Kinks, "Dedicated Follower of Fashion," 1966

The Temptations

Prince

Paul Revere and the Raiders

The Ruffled Shirt

WHO

Ray Davies, Paul Revere and the Raiders, Beau Brummel, Albert Finney (as Tom Jones), Tom Jones (as Tom Jones), Prince.

WHAT

A shirt so formal it requires only a bow tie, now frequently worn without for a decadent rock and roll look. Comes with wing or straight collar, buttons or buttonholes for studs, French cuffs. Worn underneath a jacket, the shirt fronts command center stage whether they are decorated with plain cotton bibs, vertical pleats, flattened horizontal loops, or fanciful ruffles.

WHEN

After noon at a formal wedding, after six at a black-tie event, after hours at a club (ditch the tie and undo a few buttons).

WHERE

In a Vegas lounge, in a rock video, at a party, at the altar.

HOW

Tucked into leather pants, hanging out with jeans, under a black jacket, with a tux.

WHY

To conform to formality, to confound normality.

IN 1974, WHEN MY **HAIR** WAS AT ITS LONGEST EVER, I WENT TO THE PAUL MCGREGOR SALON ON ST. MARKS PLACE, WHICH IS NOW A CLUB CALLED CONEY ISLAND HIGH. IT WAS A ROCK AND ROLL HAIR FACTORY. EVERYBODY WOULD WALK IN WITH REALLY LONG HAIR AND WALK OUT WITH A COIF. I GOT A SHAG AND IT WAS LITERALLY STANDING UP ON TOP.

David Cassidy

THE HAIR KING

When Elvis dyed his hair blue-black and slicked it down with Royal Crown pomade, TIME magazine called it "five inches of buttered yak wool." It was reduced to a flattop on March 25, 1958, when he joined the military, and did not regain its theatrical magnificence until the late sixties when the King made a TV special in which he appeared in black leather and rakish sideburns.

HAIRCUTS WE REMEMBER

Robert De Niro's mohawk in TAXI DRIVER

David Bowie's Ziggy cut

Mick Jagger in PERFORMANCE

Dirk Bogarde in VICTIM, and blond in MODESTY BLAISE

Johnny Rotten's punk cut

Brad Pitt's vertical 'do in JOHNNY SUEDE

Ed "Kookie" Byrnes on 77 Sunset Strip

Troy Donoghue in PARRISH

Michael Jackson's Jheri curls
    (inspired by Little Richard)

James Brown's pompadour

Tina Turner's PRIVATE DANCER fright wig

Diana Ross's recent extensions

Any Elvis Presley hairstyle

Roger Daltrey's TOMMY mane

Shaun Cassidy's feathered shag

Marc Bolan's ringlets

A Flock of Seagulls

New-wave wedge

Big hair

George Clooney's Caesar

David Lee Roth's shifting hairline
    (a movable feast)

Rod Stewart's Maggie Mae

Jimi Hendrix's Afro

Joey Ramone's bangs

Jethro Tull's (Ian Anderson) thick-as-a-brick mane

Bob Marley's dreads

Janis Joplin's frizz

Keanu Reeves's SPEED buzz cut

Ricky Nelson's waterfall

Yul Brynner's chrome dome

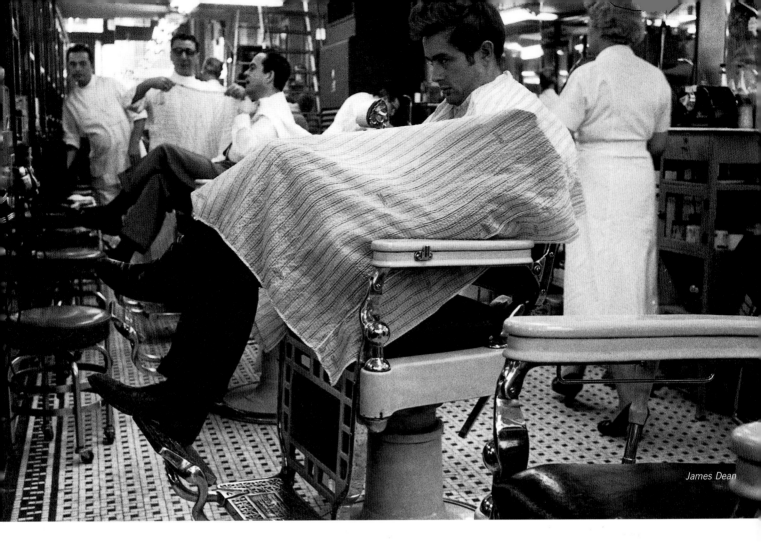

James Dean

Barbershop specials: Crew cut Flattop Brush cut Short back and sides Businessman's cut Cue ball Box and fade Mop top Pudding bowl Prince Valiant Rave mop Pompadour Military buzz Dork knob (smallish ponytail) Ponytail Braid Mohawk Mohican Center-part Suedehead Afro Jheri curl Cornrows Ducktail D.A. Dreadlocks Caesar Shag Rooster cut Spike

Little Richard

Twiggy

David Crosby

Sly Stone

After the Beatles, long hair made you cool. It could be straight, curly, a big Afro, as long as it was long.

When I was in high school, facial hair was absolutely outlawed. In the fifties and sixties, only beatniks, radicals, and Uncle Sam wore goatees.

Thelonious Monk

Malcolm X

Don Sullivan in The Rebel Set, *1959*

WHILE THE BRITISH INVASION WAS TAKING HOLD, THE CALIFORNIA **SURF SCENE** EMERGED AS A TRULY AMERICAN PHENOMENON, WITH ITS OWN LANGUAGE IN MUSIC AND FASHION. TO ME THIS WAS EXOTIC AND HOMEGROWN AT THE SAME TIME.

Jan and Dean

Surfin' Safaris

The Beach Boys—brothers Carl, Dennis, and Brian Wilson—began playing in high school with their cousin Mike Love and school friend Alan Jardine. In the beginning they were known as the Pendletons, a name they took from their favorite plaid shirts. Later they adopted striped T-shirts and surfer shirts (solid-colored, short-sleeved shirts with white piping around the neck and placket), the predominant style of the surfin' sixties. Despite their name, only one Beach Boy, Dennis, was a serious surfer; tragically, he drowned in 1983 and was buried at sea.

THE OLD-WAVE SURF BANDS: Jan and Dean   Dave Myers and the Surftones   The Bel-Airs   The Rumblers   The Chantays
The Pyramids   The Surfaris   The Rhythm Rockers   Jim Waller and the Deltas   The Lively Ones   The Surf Stompers   The Impacts
The Challengers   The Astronauts   The Ventures   The Impacts   The Crossfires (later became the Turtles)   The Tornadoes
Bob Vaught and the Renegades   The Vulcanes   Eddie and the Snowmen

Surf Life

Phil Edwards, Wind & Sea, Hang Ten, Greg Noll,
and Bing surfboards

Pontiac GTOs, woody station wagons, Ford Mustangs

Fender guitars and amps—Leo Fender, a
manufacturer from Fullerton, California, provided
and sponsored many local musicians with equipment
and consequently became responsible for the popular
surf sound

Made-in-Hawaii Hawaiian shirts

Katin Jams and Bermuda shorts in copper brown,
light blue, turquoise, red, usually with floral designs
and piping

Hang Ten shirts—broad-striped T-shirts with
embroidered feet logos

Revell model kits—created by hot-rod artist Ed "Big
Daddy" Roth, these cartoonish car kits included the
Weird-Ohs, Rat-Fink, and Freaky-Rider series

Coppertone suntan lotion

Surfspeak

CLAMBAKE
A surf party.

CRUNCHER
Hard-breaking big wave that folds over, almost impossible to ride.

DUNE BUGGY
Usually a Volkswagen engine constructed with a go-cart frame and beer keg tanks (great for weekends in Pismo Beach); popularity peaked in late sixties.

GREMMY
From Gremlin, meaning hanger-on or beginner, a pest to surfers.

HANGING 5
Five toes over the nose (front of the board).

HEAVIES
Very big waves, 18- to 20-feet high, found in Hawaii.

HO-DAD
Great, showy performer on the board.

PIPELINE
Very big "tube."

SHOREBREAK
Small waves that break close to the shore.

SPINNER
Full 360-degree turn while riding a wave, very difficult.

10 OVER
Ten toes over the nose.

TUBE
Hollow part of the wave.

The Endless Summer II, *1994*

IN THE SIXTIES, THE **PREPPY** LOOK WAS EVERYWHERE—
MY THREE SONS HAD IT; SO DID DUSTIN HOFFMAN IN *THE
GRADUATE*. IT WAS A REFINED, EDUCATED LOOK, THE LOOK OF
OLD MONEY, AND YET IT WAS COMFORTABLE. EVEN TODAY, IT'S
FOR THE PERSON WHO REALLY DOESN'T HAVE TO WEAR
ANYTHING FASHIONABLE OR SHOWY TO BE SMART. IT WORKS IN
EVERY CORNER OF THE WORLD, BUT WE'VE TURNED IT INTO AN

My Three Sons TV show

Dick Van Dyke and Mary Tyler Moore

Dustin Hoffman in The Graduate, 1967

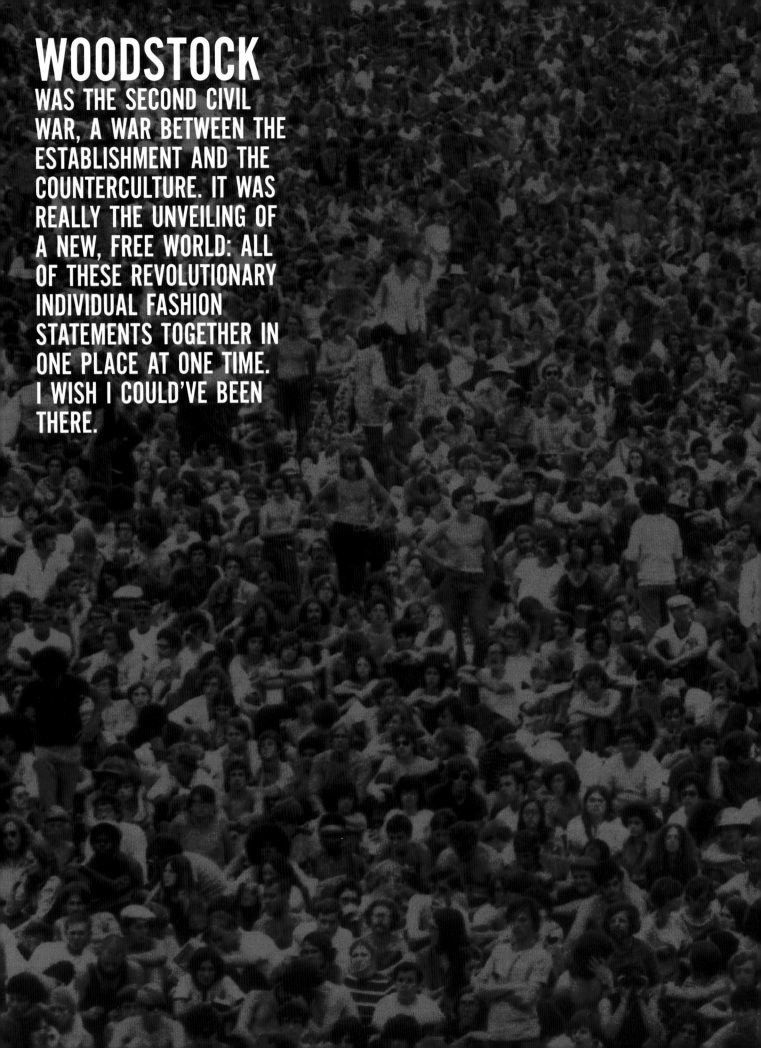

WOODSTOCK

WAS THE SECOND CIVIL
WAR, A WAR BETWEEN THE
ESTABLISHMENT AND THE
COUNTERCULTURE. IT WAS
REALLY THE UNVEILING OF
A NEW, FREE WORLD: ALL
OF THESE REVOLUTIONARY
INDIVIDUAL FASHION
STATEMENTS TOGETHER IN
ONE PLACE AT ONE TIME.
I WISH I COULD'VE BEEN
THERE.

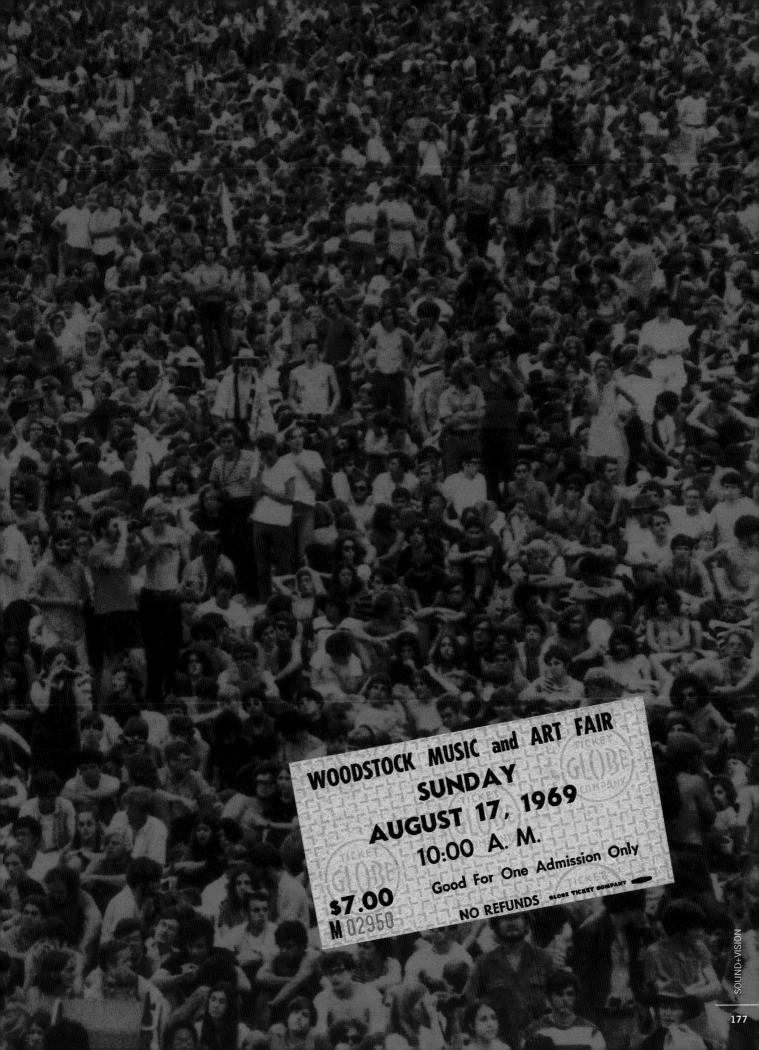

WOODSTOCK MUSIC and ART FAIR
SUNDAY
AUGUST 17, 1969
10:00 A. M.
Good For One Admission Only
$7.00
M 02950
NO REFUNDS   GLOBE TICKET COMPANY

Eddie Floyd

'57 vintage Strat

Eric Clapton

Buddy Guy

Bonnie Raitt

Jeff Beck

Yngwie Malmsteen

Richie Sambora

The Fender Stratocaster

Rock's shapeliest accessory

In 1954, the Fender Guitar Company of Fullerton, California, created the first Stratocaster. It was designed by Leo Fender, Freddie Tavares, and Bill Curson to fill a growing demand for an easy-to-play guitar, one that allowed for a freer range of movement onstage than the earlier, boxy electric guitars. The Stratocaster's biggest advantage was its body—shaved in back to contour to the player's body, with well-balanced "twin horns," and good neck-to-body ratio. It was also the first electric guitar to have three pickups, a tone-control switch, and a tremolo, or vibrato, bar. The original Stratocaster was dark sunburst, off-white, or blond with a maple neck (future versions had a neck of rosewood). Since its creation, it has been the most popular electric guitar ever made. Eric Clapton has said, "It's about as close to perfect as a guitar can be."

Buddy Holly and the Crickets

Dick Dale and the Deltones

Gene Vincent and the Blue Caps

The Beach Boys

Bill Haley and His Comets

Ritchie Valens

George Harrison

Keith Richards

Jimi Hendrix

Ry Cooder

Stevie Ray Vaughan

Ritchie Blackmore

Albert Lee

Robert Cray

Richie Sambora

Jeff Beck

Eric Clapton

Bonnie Raitt

Mark Knopfler

Nile Rodgers

Jeff Lynne

Steve Miller

Dweezil Zappa

Jimi Hendrix

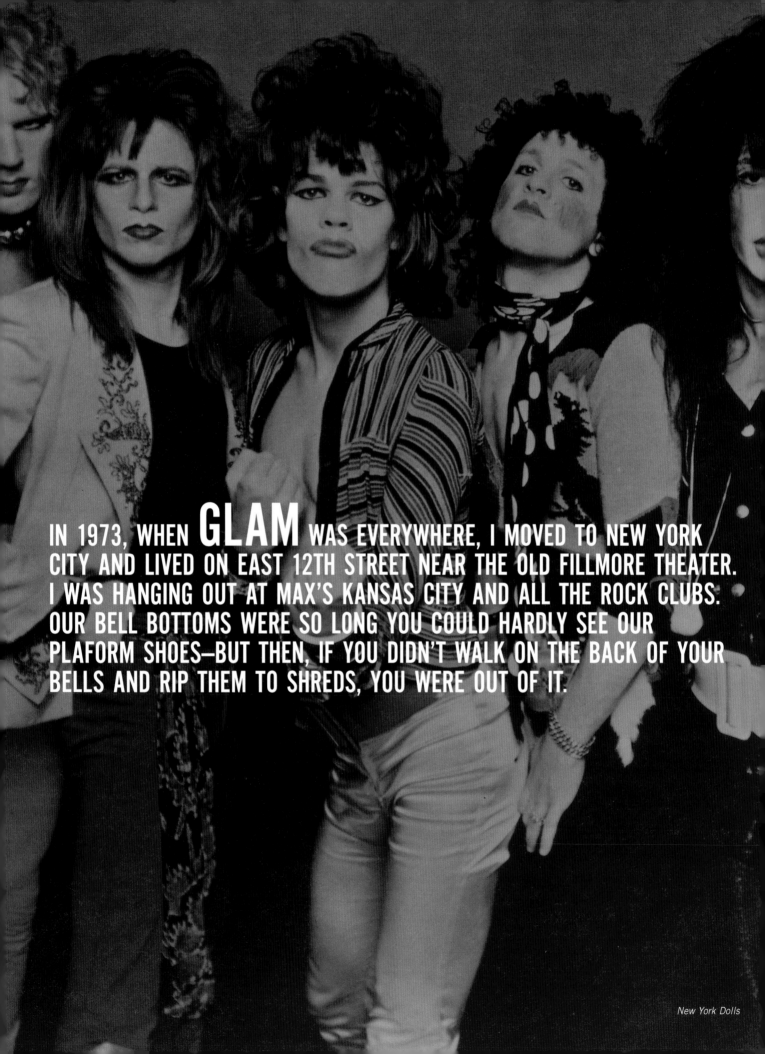

IN 1973, WHEN **GLAM** WAS EVERYWHERE, I MOVED TO NEW YORK CITY AND LIVED ON EAST 12TH STREET NEAR THE OLD FILLMORE THEATER. I WAS HANGING OUT AT MAX'S KANSAS CITY AND ALL THE ROCK CLUBS. OUR BELL BOTTOMS WERE SO LONG YOU COULD HARDLY SEE OUR PLAFORM SHOES—BUT THEN, IF YOU DIDN'T WALK ON THE BACK OF YOUR BELLS AND RIP THEM TO SHREDS, YOU WERE OUT OF IT.

New York Dolls

avid Bowie

Marc Bolan

ss

he Sweet

UNDONE TO THE NAVEL

Putting the sex into unisex

Earrings

Spandex

Feather boas

Striped poor-boy shirts

Thigh-high boots

Velvet bell bottoms

Anything in Lurex and lamé

Silver leather

Gold leather

Eye shadow

Hennaed hair

Girls' blouses

Opera gloves

Snakeskin boots

Bump-toe and platform shoes

Costume jewelry

Studded T-shirts

Lightning bolts and stars

Enormous belts

Chain belts

Silk scarves

Hip-huggers

Satin anything

Sequins

Glitter

LIKE EVERY PREPPY KID, THE **SHOES** I GREW UP WEARING WERE WHITE BUCKS WITH BRICK RED SOLES, JUST LIKE THE KIND PAT BOONE WORE, AND I WEAR THEM TO THIS DAY. BUT WHEN IT CAME TO GLAMOUR, NOTHING FIT BETTER THAN A PAIR OF HIGH-HEELED SNAKESKIN BOOTS.

Seventies snakeskin boots.
Photograph by Bill Steele

Pat Boone and his white bucks

Nancy Sinatra and her boots

Carl Perkins without his blue suede shoes

Shoe Biz

In the beginning, rock and roll made a point. So did rock and roll shoes, from R&B's shiny black oxfords to Carl Perkins's blue suede shoes. When rock went "white bread," Pat Boone made white bucks and round-toed saddle shoes popular. Then came the Beatles, who refashioned ankle-high Chelsea boots into pointy-toed boots with stacked Cuban heels. In the late sixties and seventies, rock shoes made big news with platform soles and bulbous "bump toes," and boots went thigh-high. Mick Jagger, who had been hanging out with ballet greats Nureyev and Baryshnikov, wore Capezio jazz oxfords onstage in 1975, starting a trend that was revived in the eighties by such British New Romantics as Duran Duran. Punk revitalized the fifties crepe-sole suede shoe (also known as a "brothel creeper") and introduced Doc Martens to the world. In the nineties, Docs still rule, while rappers and latter-day punks have embraced classic sneakers and high-tech high tops as their footwear of choice.

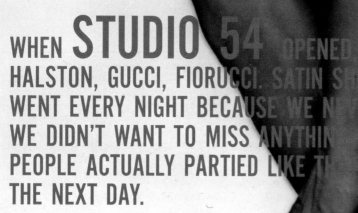

WHEN **STUDIO 54** OPENED IT WAS A REAL BUZZ. HALSTON, GUCCI, FIORUCCI. SATIN SHIRTS AND DESIGNER JEANS. WE WENT EVERY NIGHT BECAUSE WE NEVER KNEW WHAT TO EXPECT AND WE DIDN'T WANT TO MISS ANYTHING. IT'S HARD TO IMAGINE NOW THAT PEOPLE ACTUALLY PARTIED LIKE THAT AND WERE ABLE TO FUNCTION THE NEXT DAY.

Now everybody can get into Studio 54.

Jeans advertisement. Photograph by Gordon Munro

Liza Minnelli, Halston, and Steve Rubell

David Geffen and Joni Mitchell

...and Michael Jackson

Andy Warhol, Debbie Harry, and Grace Jones

Polyester

In England, just after World War II, J. T. Dickson and J. R. Whinfield of the Calico Printers Association devised a way to spin molten polymers—giant molecules created by combining elements from coal and petroleum—into threads, creating the first polyester fiber. DuPont purchased the patents in 1950 and 1952, coining the term "wash and wear" to describe a blend of cotton and acrylic. Polyester was first produced in mass quantities in 1953.

Early polyesters were called modacrylic, Acrilan, Dynel, Orlon, and Chromspun. Nice, but spongy and impenetrable, with problems holding dyes. As technology advanced, polyester became refined enough to imitate wool, down, suede, silk, or rubber, depending on how the chemicals were processed. Polyester seemed a miracle fabric, holding its color and shape in perpetuity and requiring virtually no care.

In the early seventies, to compete with the "natural" backlash, the evil synthetic fiber took on such trade names as Kodel, Fortel, Crepesoft, and Golden Touch. And by 1974 double-knit polyester ruled the world: leisure suits, pantsuits, slacks, and shirts in fab textures, boffo colors like powder blue and terra-cotta red, fluorescent flares, and eye-poking patterns like paisley and peace symbols.

In 1977, John Travolta made polyester history in his white SATURDAY NIGHT FEVER suit. By the eighties, however, polyester was deemed gauche; synthetic microfibers were in. But that was just gilding the lily. By the end of the nineties, tight, wildly patterned polyester clothes—or polyester mixed with cotton and Lycra in athletic clothes—became the most fashionable clothes on the club scene.

Disco Duds

DAY	NIGHT
A. Smile	Fiorucci
Bonhomme	Gucci
Pierre Cardin	Halston
Faded Glory	Charles Jourdan
Gentleman John	Kenzo
Huk-A-Poo	Nik Nik
Landlubber	Pucci
Michael Millea	Gloria Vanderbilt
Flo Toronto	Diane Von Furstenberg
Truth & Soul	Claude Montana
Viceroy	Jordache
Billy Whiskers	Sasson
	Bonjour
	Willi Wear
	Thierry Mugler

A GROUP OF YOUNG PEOPLE DECIDED TO PUT OUT MESSAGES OF LIFE IN A RHYTHMIC WAY. NOW A LEGITIMATE FORM OF EXPRESSION, **HIP-HOP** CONTINUES TO MAKE HISTORY. IT ALL BEGAN AS A RESULT OF THE YOUTH CULTURE EMBRACING AND WEARING STATUS SYMBOLS, DESIGNER LABELS, AND ATHLETIC NAMES AND WEAVING THEM INTO THEIR TESTIMONY. THE COMMUNITY HAS BEEN AND CONTINUES TO BE AN INSPIRATION TO ME—HOW I LOOK AT FASHION AND DESIGN FOR THE YOUNG PEOPLE.

The Fugees. Photographed by Matthew Rolston

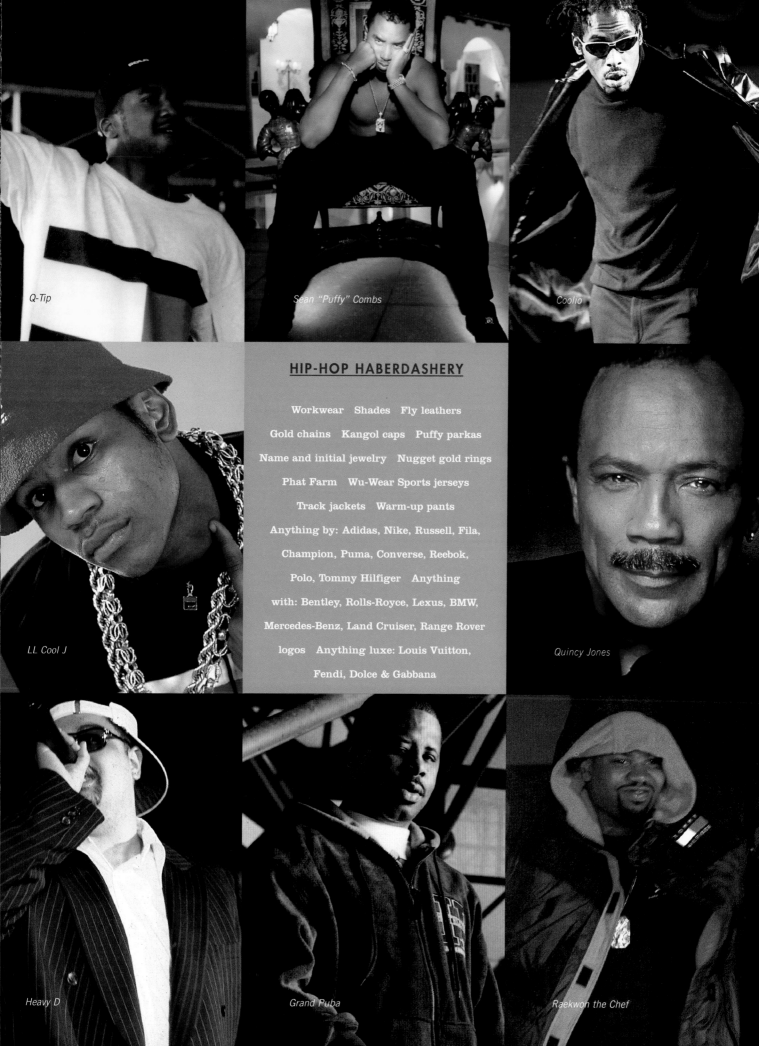

Q-Tip

Sean "Puffy" Combs

Coolio

HIP-HOP HABERDASHERY

Workwear   Shades   Fly leathers

Gold chains   Kangol caps   Puffy parkas

Name and initial jewelry   Nugget gold rings

Phat Farm   Wu-Wear Sports jerseys

Track jackets   Warm-up pants

Anything by: Adidas, Nike, Russell, Fila,

Champion, Puma, Converse, Reebok,

Polo, Tommy Hilfiger   Anything

with: Bentley, Rolls-Royce, Lexus, BMW,

Mercedes-Benz, Land Cruiser, Range Rover

logos   Anything luxe: Louis Vuitton,

Fendi, Dolce & Gabbana

LL Cool J

Quincy Jones

Heavy D

Grand Puba

Raekwon the Chef

THE **ALTERNATIVE** LOOK IS A COMBINATION OF MUSICAL AND VISUAL STYLES INFLUENCED BY SKATEBOARDING, PUNK ROCK, HEAVY METAL, AND RAP. IT'S AN ANTI-FASHION STATEMENT THAT HAS DEVELOPED INTO ITS OWN FORM OF CHIC BY DRAGGING WELL-WORN AMERICAN CLASSICS OUT OF THE CLOSETS AND THRIFT SHOPS AND ONTO THE ROCK AND ROLL STAGE.

grunge is dead

Kurt Cobain

THE ALTERNATIVE ESSENTIALS

Essential alternatives from A to X

Adidas

Airwalk

Baby-doll dresses

Backpacks

Baggy butt jeans

Baseball caps

Ben Sherman shirts

Black Flys

Body piercing

Boxer shorts

Carolina boots

Caterpillar boots

Converse One Stars

Dee Cee

Dickies

Doc Martens

Earrings

Flannel

Georgia Giants boots

Goatees

Heavy-metal T-shirts

Jams

Milkfed clothes

Mohair sweaters

Muscle cars

Nail polish

Oakleys

Pocket watches

Red Wing boots

Tattoos

Thermal (waffle-weave) underwear

Too-big and too-small shirts

Underground comics

Vans

Watch caps

Wallets with chains

X-Girl

X-Large

EVERYONE WANTS TO BE IDENTIFIED AS PART OF A CERTAIN GROUP OR **TRIBE.** I THINK PEOPLE PERCEIVE THEMSELVES AS BEING A CERTAIN TYPE AND THEN FOLLOW THAT TO THE ABSOLUTE. THEY BECOME FANATICAL ABOUT HOW THEY LOOK AND HOW THEY DRESS AND GO TO GREAT LENGTHS TO BECOME THIS PARTICULAR PERSON. SO THEIR CHOICE OF CLOTHING, HAIRCUTS, SHOES, GLASSES, JEWELRY, CASUAL WEAR, UNDERWEAR, AS WELL AS WHERE THEY GO AND HOW THEY GET THERE, IS ALL WRAPPED UP INTO THEIR PSYCHOLOGICAL BEING.

West Side Story, 1961

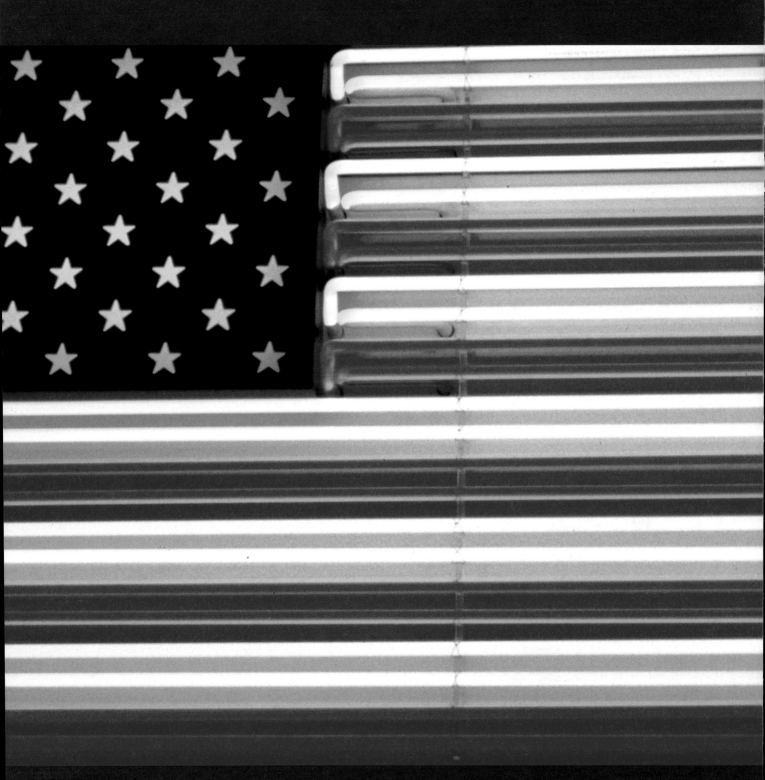

Putting this book together, compiling my memories of growing up, my thoughts about America, my ideas about the way we live, has made me realize that style is nothing less than the way we carve out our existence. It is what we like and what we don't, the things that make our hearts beat faster and make us feel comfortable. It is our individual eccentricities and our common interests.

Today we live in a society composed of different tribes and customs. Pop culture is our common denominator. It comprises people, places, ideas, and objects that constantly influence each other, causing new hybrids in style. There is music-inspired fashion and pop songs about shopping and runway models. There are products designed to look like Warhol paintings and TV commercials that push the frontiers of filmmaking in 60 seconds or less. Hip-hop fans adopt preppy fashions while suburban kids borrow looks and ideas from urban kids. Appropriation has become an art form in itself. We work and speak in a language that is derived from many cultural sources. We are equal-opportunity employers of a vast, ever changing world of personal styles.

I see this trade-off taking place, and it motivates me to do new, innovative things. I can take ideas from the past or from the future and put them together in a meaningful way for tomorrow. Anything is possible. After all, I have been through 40 years of cultural change, from Ozzie and Harriet to Nirvana and the Notorious B.I.G. I have experienced the excitement of being young and reckless and all the contentment of becoming a successful businessman and a happy, loving family man. I still get a rush every time I hear Pete Townshend strike a chord or listen to Run DMC rap about their Adidas. And, in my own way, I believe I am as much a producer of pop culture as I am a product of it.

I wouldn't have it any other way. The way Americans dress and work and play has become a standard for the rest of the world. And with technology opening new doors every day, the world is getting smaller every day. Style is still a highly personal quality, but it is one that causes ripples throughout the world. With the World Wide Web, e-mail, and digital TV, it is only natural that we will develop new cultural icons that will expand our understanding of style and our expression of it. As the culture changes, I've found that fashion is just one means of communication, so it's time to explore the world of style from the inside out with TV, video, books like this, music, and the Internet. As a man of pop culture, I hope to continue to investigate how it works, how ideas and images can be put together, taken apart, and reassembled. I want to learn who sets the styles and how it all comes about. And what it all means.

Photography credits: All illustrations are copyrighted © the individual photographers and artists and/or reprinted by permission of the resources listed below.

Page ii: H. Armstrong Roberts. Page v: Courtesy of Hofstra University. Pages vi–vii: Courtesy of Hofstra University. Page viii, left to right: The Bettmann Archive; courtesy of Chuck Davis/Ernie Davis: The Elmira Express—The Story of a Heisman Trophy Winner, Bartleby Press, 1983; courtesy of Tommy Hilfiger. INTRODUCTION Page 3: John Margolies Collection. Page 5, clockwise from top left: Corbis-Bettmann; R. Kravette, Jericho, NY/courtesy of Schwinn; courtesy of Tommy Hilfiger; the Bettmann Archive; Archive Photos; courtesy of the Varsity, Inc., 61 North Ave., Atlanta, GA. Page 6: Photofest. Page 7: Wayne Miller/Magnum Photos, Inc. Page 8: © Walt Disney Productions/Photofest. Page 10, top to bottom: Courtesy of Tommy Hilfiger; R. Kravette, Jericho, NY/used with permission of the Procter & Gamble Company; © 1963 Bristol-Myers, reproduced with permission of the Bristol-Myers Squibb Company. Page 11: Courtesy of Tommy Hilfiger. Page 12: The Endless Summer poster: John Van Hamersveld/reprinted with permission of Bruce Brown; Woodstock poster: Art of Rock; copyright © The Star-Gazette, Elmira, NY, reprinted with permission, all rights reserved. Page 13: Courtesy of Tommy Hilfiger. Page 15: Peter Gridley/FPG International. AMERICANA Page 16: Joseph H. Bailey/copyright © National Geographic Society. Page 18, left to right: David Noble/FPG International; W. Bertsch/H. Armstrong Roberts; R. Kord/H. Armstrong Roberts. Page 20: Steve Edson/Photonica. Page 21: Peter Gridley/FPG International. Pages 22–25: Printed by permission of the Norman Rockwell Family Trust, copyright © 1947 the Norman Rockwell Family Trust. Photos courtesy of the Norman Rockwell Museum at Stockbridge, MA. Page 26: Andreas Feininger/Life magazine, © Time, Inc. Page 27: Bill Steele. Page 28: Elliott Erwitt/Magnum Photos, Inc. Page 29: From Thomas Hine, Populuxe, the Karpfinger Agency, 1986. Pages 30–31: Norman Mauskopf/Matrix. Page 32: Kurt Markus. Page 33, clockwise from top left: Photofest; Photofest; Springer/Corbis-Bettmann; Photofest. Pages 34–35: Bill Steele. Page 36: Courtesy of R. P. Nadeau, Moose River Trading Co., Inc., Thendara, NY. Page 37: Bill Steele. Page 38: Lambert/Archive Photos. Page 39: David Bashaw. Page 40: H. Armstrong Roberts. Page 41: R. Kravette, Jericho, NY/used with permission of Heinz USA. Page 42: David Bashaw; inset: Kobal Collection. Page 43: H. Armstrong Roberts. CLASSICS Page 44: Jack Zwillenger/Michael Ochs Archives/Venice, CA, and courtesy of Rhino Entertainment Company. Page 46: Costa Manos/Magnum Photos, Inc. Pages 48–49: UPI/Corbis-Bettmann. Pages 50–51: David Bashaw. Pages 52–55: Bill Steele/courtesy of Starstruck, New York. Pages 56–57: David Bashaw; inset: Corbis-Bettmann. Page 58: Kobal Collection. Page 59: Pollack-Krasner House and Study Center, East Hampton, NY/© Estate of Hans Namuth. Pages 60–61: Eve Arnold/Magnum Photos, Inc. Page 62, top to bottom: Kobal Collection; Cornell Capa/Magnum Photos, Inc. Page 63: Photofest. Page 64: Courtesy of Jockey International Inc. Archives. Page 65: Kobal Collection; underwear illustrations by Tom Davidson. Pages 66–67: Cornell Capa/Magnum Photos, Inc. Pages 68–69: Bill Steele/courtesy of Fools and Horses, Brooklyn, NY. Page 70: H. Armstrong Roberts. Page 71: Elliott Erwitt/Magnum Photos, Inc. Pages 72–73: Bill Steele. Pages 74–75: Kobal Collection. Page 76: Kobal Collection. Page 77: Archive Photos. Page 78: H. Armstrong Roberts. Page 79: Bill Steele. Page 80: Thomas Oatman Collection. Page 81: H. Armstrong Roberts. Page 82: David Bashaw. Page 83: Wayne Miller/Magnum Photos, Inc. Page 84: UPI/Corbis-Bettmann. Page 85: H. Armstrong Roberts. Page 86: UPI/Corbis-Bettmann. Page 87: Photofest; inset: Quintet Publishing Ltd. Pages 88–89: Kobal Collection. Page 90: Bill Steele. Page 91: 45th Infantry Archives. Page 93: Photofest. Pages 94–95, left to right: Kobal Collection; Kobal Collection; Photofest; Corbis-Bettmann; Kobal Collection; Kobal Collection; suit time-line illustrations by Tom Davidson. Pages 96–97: Private collection. The Gulf trademark is owned by the Chevron Corporation. Page 98: Bill Steele. Page 99: Gas-station logos: John Margolies/Esto; Mobilgas: John Margolies Collection/reproduced with permission from Mobil Oil Corporation; The Jerk: Photofest. Pages 100–101: Kobal Collection. Page 102: Courtesy of MPTV. Page 103, clockwise from top left: Ron Stoner/Surfer magazine; Kobal Collection; courtesy of Jantzen Inc.; Archive Photos. Pages 104–105: Bill Steele. Page 106, inset, top to bottom: Photofest; Kobal Collection. Pages 106–107: Photofest. Page 108: David Bashaw. Page 109, clockwise from top left: Photofest; Photofest; Photofest; Photofest; courtesy of the International Tennis Hall of Fame, Newport, RI; Michael Ochs Archives/Venice, CA; Photofest; Archive Photos. ATHLETICS Page 110: Archive Photos. Page 112, left to right: Underwood & Underwood/Corbis-Bettmann; courtesy of Chuck Davis/Ernie Davis: The Elmira Express—The Story of a Heisman Trophy Winner, Bartleby Press, 1983. Page 114: Courtesy of Abbeville Press/Thomas Steele. Page 115: AMF Bowling, Inc. Pages 116–117: Archive Photos. Page 118: Robert Knudsen, White House/John F. Kennedy Library, Boston, MA. Page 119: Daniel Forster Photography. Pages 120–121: Burt Glinn/Magnum Photos, Inc. Page 122, background: Courtesy of Purdue University Book Store, Inc.; top to bottom: Courtesy of UCLA; courtesy of JFK High School, Woodbridge Township School District, NJ; courtesy of Athens State College, Athens, GA; courtesy of Colonial Heights High School, Richmond, VA; courtesy of Pace University. Page 123: NFL Photos. Pages 124–125: Robert Riger/courtesy of James Danziger Gallery. Page 126: Photofest. Page 127: UPI/Corbis-Bettmann. Page 128: Theo Westenberger/Gamma Liaison Network. Page 129: UPI/Corbis-Bettmann. Pages 130–131: Bill Steele. Pages 132–133: H. Armstrong Roberts. Page 134: UPI/Corbis-Bettmann. Page 135: Courtesy of the International Tennis Hall of Fame, Newport, RI. Page 136: Bill Steele. Page 137, top, left to right: David Taylor/AllSport; David Taylor/AllSport; Pascal Rondeau/AllSport; Pascal Rondeau/AllSport; Mike Powell/AllSport; bottom: Courtesy of Tommy Hilfiger. Pages 138–139: Bill Steele/courtesy of What Goes Around Comes Around, New York. Page 140: Converse, Inc. Page 141: Jonathan Daniel/AllSport. Page 142: Lambert/Archive Photos. Page 143: Greg Miller Photography. Page 144: H. Armstrong Roberts. Page 145, inset: Michael Ochs Archives/Venice, CA. Page 145: H. Armstrong Roberts. SOUND+VISION Page 146: Archive Photos. Page 148: Wayne Miller/Magnum Photos, Inc. Page 150, left to right: Alice Ochs/Michael Ochs Archives/Venice, CA; Kriegsmann/Michael Ochs Archives/Venice, CA; E. C. Winters/Steve La Vere Photographs. Page 151: Dezo/Michael Ochs Archives/Venice, CA. Pages 152–153: Photofest. Page 154, left to right: Michael Ochs Archives/Venice, CA; Archive Photos; UPI/Corbis-Bettmann. Page 155: Michael Ochs Archives/Venice, CA. Page 156: Michael Ochs Archives/Venice, CA. Page 157, clockwise from left: Photofest; Michael Ochs Archives/Venice, CA; Don Paulsen/Michael Ochs Archives/Venice, CA. Pages 158–159: Sid Avery/MPTV. Page 160: Photofest. Page 161, clockwise from top left: Archive Photos; Kobal Collection; MPTV; Photofest. Page 162: Michael Ochs Archives/Venice, CA. Page 163: Harry Goodwin/Michael Ochs Archives/Venice, CA. Page 164: Harry Goodwin/Michael Ochs Archives/Venice, CA. Page 165, top to bottom: Don Paulsen/Michael Ochs Archives/Venice, CA; Photofest; Photofest. Page 166: Photofest. Page 167, top to bottom: UPI/Corbis-Bettmann; Michael Ochs Archives/Venice, CA. Page 168, top: Dennis Stock/Magnum Photos, Inc.; bottom, left to right: Michael Ochs Archives/Venice, CA; Archive Photos/LDE; Michael Ochs Archives/Venice, CA; Michael Ochs Archives/Venice, CA. Page 169, top: Archive Photos; bottom, clockwise from left: Photofest; Lee Tanner/Photography; Archive Photos/American Stock; Archive Photos/Express Newspapers. Page 170: Michael Ochs Archives/Venice, CA. Page 171: Michael Ochs Archives/Venice, CA. Page 172: Surfer magazine. Page 173: Aaron Chang/MPTV . Page 174: Kobal Collection. Page 175, clockwise from top left: Kobal Collection; Photofest; Kobal Collection. Pages 175–176: Amalie Rothschild-Corbis-Bettmann; inset: Art of Rock. Page 178: Courtesy of Fender. Page 179: Jill Gibson/Michael Ochs Archives/Venice, CA. Page 180: Michael Ochs Archives/Venice, CA. Page 181, clockwise from top left: Lynn Goldsmith/LGI Photo Agency; Michael Ochs Archives/Venice, CA; Michael Ochs Archives/Venice, CA; Harry Goodwin/Michael Ochs Archives/Venice, CA. Page 182: Bill Steele. Page 183, top to bottom: Michael Ochs Archives/Venice, CA; Photofest; Michael Ochs Archives/Venice, CA. Page 184: Gordon Munro. Page 185: Gamma Liaison Network. Page 186: Matthew Rolston. Page 187, clockwise from top left: Steve Eichner; Michael Benabib; Dan Lecca; Greg Gorman; Dan Lecca; courtesy of Elektra Records; Dan Lecca; Janette Beckman/Retna Pictures. Page 188: Stephen Sweet/Retna Pictures. Page 189: Ian Tilton/Retna Pictures. Pages 190–191: Penguin/Corbis-Bettmann. Page 192: Stephen G. St. John/copyright © National Geographic Society. Pages 193–194, first row, left to right: Kobal Collection; Converse, Inc.; Bill Steele; Burt Glinn/Magnum Photos, Inc.; Bill Steele; Photofest; Art of Rock; © Walt Disney Productions/Photofest; second row: John F. Kennedy Library, Boston, MA; Kobal Collection; David Bashaw; Archive Photos; UPI/Corbis-Bettmann; Michael Ochs Archives/Venice, CA; courtesy of Jockey International Inc. Archives; Theo Westenberger/Gamma Liaison Network; third row: Elliott Erwitt/Magnum Photos, Inc.; Jill Gibson/Michael Ochs Archives/Venice, CA; Kobal Collection; Lambert/Archive Photos; 45th Infantry Archives; courtesy of Tommy Hilfiger; courtesy of Abbeville Press/Thomas Steele; H. Armstrong Roberts; fourth row: UPI/Corbis-Bettmann; courtesy of R. P. Nadeau, Moose River Trading Co., Inc., Thendara, NY; courtesy of Tommy Hilfiger; Michael Ochs Archives/Venice, CA; Kobal Collection; courtesy of Tommy Hilfiger; Cornell Capa/Magnum Photos, Inc.; courtesy of Hofstra University. Page 196: Courtesy of Hofstra University. "Dedicated Follower of Fashion" written by Ray Davies © 1966, renewed 1994 ABKCO Music, Inc. & Warner/Chappell Music, all rights reserved, reprinted by permission, © 1966 (renewed) Davray Music Ltd. (PRS), administered by Unichappell Music, Inc. (BMI), all rights reserved, used by permission. ADDITIONAL ACKNOWLEDGMENTS Editorial associates: Nadine Hwa, Orville Kiser, Robin Maltz, Samuel Pizarro II, Anne Marie Purdy, Maura Reilly, and Tara Rodgers. Additional research and writing: Charles Cermele, Jeff Indusi, Lance Loud, Seven McDonald, Katy McNerny, Stephen Saban, Rachel Small, and Mike Vague. Additional picture research: John Clarke, Ari Form, and Ana Ossowski.